W9-BAC-709

CULTURES IN CONFLICT

CULTURES
IN CONFLICT

*Social Movements
and the State in Peru*

SUSAN C. STOKES

UNIVERSITY OF CALIFORNIA PRESS
BERKELEY   LOS ANGELES   LONDON

This book is a print-on-demand volume. It is manufactured using toner in place of ink. Type and images may be less sharp than the same material seen in traditionally printed University of California Press editions.

University of California Press
Berkeley and Los Angeles, California

University of California Press, Ltd.
London, England

© 1995 by
The Regents of the University of California

Library of Congress Cataloging-in-Publication Data
Stokes, Susan Carol.
    Cultures in conflict : social movements and the state in
Peru / Stokes.
        p.   cm.
    Includes bibliographical references and index.
    ISBN 0–520-08617–1 (alk. paper).—ISBN 0–520-20023–3
(pbk. : alk. paper)
    Social movements—Peru. 2. Peru—Politics and
government—1980– 3. Urban poor—Peru—Political activity.
4. Social conflict—Peru. I. Title.
    HN343.5.S76 1995
303.48′4′0985—dc20   94–11496
                                                                     CIP

Printed in the United States of America

The paper used in this publication meets the minimum
requirements of American National Standard for Information
Sciences—Permanence of Paper for Printed Library Materials,
ANSI Z39.48–1984.

For my father, Donald E. Stokes,
and my mother, Sybil L. Stokes,
with love and gratitude

Not ideas, but material and ideal interests, directly govern men's conduct. Yet very frequently the "world images" that have been created by "ideas" have, like switchmen, determined the tracks along which action has been pushed by the dynamic of interest.

Max Weber

[The great mass] has, for reasons of submission and intellectual subordination, adopted a conception [of the world] which is not its own but is borrowed from another group . . . this is the conception which it follows in "normal times" . . . when its conduct is not independent and autonomous, but submissive and subordinate.

Antonio Gramsci

Contents

Figures and Tables

Figures

Tables

Preface

On July 17, 1992, eighteen hundred pounds of dynamite contained in two car bombs exploded in one of Lima's wealthiest neighborhoods, killing twenty-five people, destroying buildings, and shattering glass over a fifteen-block radius. The attack signaled Sendero Luminoso (Shining Path) guerrillas' new strategy of direct assaults on upper-class Peru; it also was intended to demonstrate the incapacity of the recently created civilian-military dictatorship, under Alberto Fujimori, to contain the guerrilla movement.

Such an attack would have been unimaginable in Peru two decades earlier. Sendero itself would have been unimaginable until relatively recently in a country that has a small Left, a labor movement cooperative with conservative governments, and a quiescent urban lower class. But in the past two decades many poor Peruvians of the cities and the countryside have taken part in social movements, most of them (unlike Sendero) peaceable. The relationship between this more common peaceful politics and the armed path of Sendero is complex; still, Sendero is an outgrowth of the same processes that have transformed much of Peru's previously passive lower classes into active agents of political change.

This book is about this transformation. I analyze how poor people in the capital city of one Latin American country overcame a history of quiescence to become active pursuers of deep political and social changes and how they came to see the political world around them in new ways. I explore the peculiar and unanticipated effects that states can have in stimulating movements of the poor, whether or not this is the intention of the political leadership. Finally, through close attention to the political, organizational, and cultural background to the rise of social movements, I address the question whether lowly actors ever consent to their subordination.

Many people, some in Peru and others in the United States, have contributed to my work. Several organizations in Independencia, the district of Lima where my fieldwork took place, offered me access to unpublished information and allowed me to observe and take part in their activities. These include three research and leadership training centers—Grupo Warmi, CIPEP, and Proceso Social—as well as UCOFAI, an organization of self-run community kitchens. Throughout the period of my fieldwork I worked closely with the staff of the Municipal Council of Independencia, under Mayor Esther Moreno (1983–89). I particularly wish to thank Lourdes Chávez and the staff of the council's Office of Neighborhood Participation.

Many individuals in Independencia contributed time and energy to carrying out a sample survey. Oscar Escate, Luis Yngaruca, Noemí Zúñiga, and Zulema Zevallos supervised a troop of about thirty young interviewers, college and high school students who were also district residents. The interviewers' task often required repeated visits to shanties built high in the hills, where many of Independencia's residents live. Both supervisors and interviewers worked with energy and good humor; their enduring friendship is among the most satisfying results of this work.

The Centro de Investigaciones of the Universidad del Pacífico, under the direction of Dr. Carlos Amat y León, graciously accepted me as a research affiliate. Luis Abugattas and Fernando Tuesta were stimulating and helpful colleagues.

A Fulbright-Hays grant made my research possible in 1985–86. I am grateful to Dr. Marcia Koth de Paredes, the Fulbright Commission of Lima, and the commission's staff for their support. The Graduate School Research Fund of the University of Washington funded a follow-up visit in 1989.

James Caporaso, José Cheibub, José Deustua, Jon Elster, Richard Fagen, Charles R. Hale, Ivan Hinojosa, Terry Karl, David Laitin, Dan Lev, Margaret Levi, John Padgett, Jorge Parodi, Adam Przeworski, Philippe Schmitter, James Scott, Donald Stokes, Michael Taylor, Kathy Teghtsoonian, and Fernando Tuesta read and commented on portions or full drafts of this study. Their criticisms and suggestions greatly enriched the book and the experience of writing it.

Part One

The State and Social Movements

Chapter One

Movements from Below, Hegemony from Above

On a warm summer day in 1985 Rosario Huayta and eighty other women descended from buses near the health ministry, on Lima's Avenida Salaverry, and saw before them a police water cannon.[1] The cannon was aimed at a protesting group of strikers outside the labor ministry, just across the street. To keep it from being trained on the new arrivals, a delegation from Huayta's group, the Feminine Committee of Communal Works of Ermitaño, approached the policemen standing guard outside the health ministry. "What do you think of that?" Huayta asked, pointing toward the strikers. "You're badly paid, you're fathers with children, and you don't even have a clinic you can take them to."

The strategy had worked in the past, and it worked again now. The police stood by as the Feminine Committee broke into two groups, one remaining outside, the other entering the ministry inconspicuously, three members at a time. The women inside, many with babies strapped to their backs in brightly colored cloth *mantas,* were indistinguishable from others like them milling about and were ignored by ministry personnel. Once upstairs, the members of the Feminine Committee gathered together, unfurled a banner, and began to shout: "A health center for Ermitaño! We demand a solution!" Hearing the chanting inside, the forty women outside joined in. "Telephones started ringing," Huayta recalled, "people stuck their heads out the windows, the whole ministry, the director included, got scared." An

3

official asked the group to stop shouting, promising that their demands would be heard. Huayta and the others insisted that he go outside and speak directly to the whole Feminine Committee. Surrounded by the women, the official offered materials to construct the health center if the community would provide the labor. "We said 'no,'" Huayta recalled. "The state had to give us the health center completed. The people don't have enough to eat, so how can you expect us to work Saturdays and Sundays also?"

Huayta's life was full of such confrontations, and not only with bureaucrats in government ministries. The equipment and medicines that the Feminine Committee eventually extracted from the health ministry were sent via a community clinic in Rímac, an area in northern Lima, where the community group in charge wanted them to remain. The Feminine Committee organized a protest outside the Rímac clinic, this time carrying empty evaporated milk cans with stones inside to make a disturbance. Even closer to home, the members of the Feminine Committee had had to overcome their husbands' objections to female activism. "Many men didn't like it. They said, 'It's all right for women to learn to read and write, but they can't go on marches.' They forbade us. But we taught the women to lose their fear of speaking in public, their fear of demanding their rights."

Who is Rosario Huayta, and what makes her thrive on a confrontational politics that many who are wealthier, better educated, better connected, and more physically imposing would shrink from? Even though for decades Peru has had one of the most skewed income distributions in the world, the politics Huayta embodies was not always common among the poor in that country. Her counterparts in an earlier era were men who would enter the ministry of health or housing with trepidation, careful not to violate implicit but well-known rules of decorum. And Huayta's politics of confrontation still are not for everyone. One of her neighbors said that he preferred "direct dealing" (*trato directo*) with his employers to membership in a union because "this way we don't go on strikes or on marches. We don't create problems or anything public."

The "making" of Rosario Huayta and many thousands of poor people like her is the central story of this book. It is the story of the transformation of politics in one Latin American country, but its themes are more universal. This particular story raises a general question: When subordinate groups do not mobilize collectively, does inaction reflect anticipated or real repression or the perception that movements would be likely to fail? Or, alternatively, does it reflect the consent of subordinate groups to the order that keeps them in positions of subordination? Many scholars argue that much inaction, rather than reflecting consent, is strategic. The Peruvian case shows that a kind of consent may lie behind relative political passivity of the poor, just as the shattering of consent may be a precondition for lower-class mobilization.

Movements and Consciousness

The question, Do the powerful keep the subordinate in line through a manipulated consent, as opposed to through repression and dependence? has worried researchers studying peasants in Malaysia, miners in Appalachia, industrial workers in Brazil, and city residents in the U.S. Middle West.[2] Although this question is frequently raised in discussions of the causes of social revolutions (see below), it can just as well be asked about less dramatic patterns of subordinate group action (or inaction). Why, for instance, might landless peasants not press for land reform? Or why might industrial workers not press for unions or the right to strike?

According to Theda Skocpol, a prominent macrohistorical sociologist, revolutionary movements from below emerge when peasants or workers perceive a crisis of the state (which lessens the likelihood of repression and increases the likelihood of success), not when their mentality becomes revolutionary.[3] Skocpol exhorts us to see social revolutions as structural events that do not rely on a revolutionary consciousness among the lower strata. She ridicules "voluntarist" views of revolutions as made by a "purposive, mass-based movement—coalescing with the aid of ideology and organization—that consciously undertakes to overthrow the existing government and perhaps the entire social order."[4] Objective features of class relations and the strength or weakness of the state explain the outbreak of revolutionary movements.

Revolutionary movements from below emerge when subordinate classes can overcome the free-rider problem and act collectively on shared interests that they have always been aware of—this is the view of several rational choice theorists.[5] Michael Taylor, for example, develops his analysis of the causes of peasant revolutions in critical dialogue with Skocpol, because he is skeptical of her view of actors as unreflective bearers of macroforces. In deciding whether to take part in revolutionary collective action, peasants will regard revolutions, if successful, as collective goods, ones they will benefit from whether or not they have contributed to their making. The tendency to free ride, to leave costly participation in revolutionary movements to others, is attenuated when peasants live in communities—places in which members hold beliefs and values in common, relations among members are direct and many-sided, and reciprocity is generalized. These qualities of community make it easier for peasants to monitor each other's behavior and apply sanctions to free riders. Given a collective interest in revolutionary change, it is varying levels of community, not varying consciousness, according to Taylor, that produce movements in some periods and quiescence in others.

Social consciousness derives, according to James Scott, from the social relations of production, only slightly tempered by the "normative context"; when the poor do not act collectively to improve their lot, they are anticipating repression or the low probability of success.[6] In his extensive study of class relations in rural Malaysia Scott attempts to demonstrate that poor peasants are by no means in the thrall of dominant ideology. Like the macrostructural sociologist Skocpol and the rational-choice theorist Taylor, Scott believes that when movements erupt, the people causing the eruption are simply aspiring to the same goals and acting on the same interests they have always aspired to and acted on.

A crisis of the state, free-rider problems in the absence of community, and the anticipation of repression or failure all have undoubtedly inhibited social movements. But recent theorists have gone too far in claiming that consent by the weak never undergirds social stability. A strand of social theory whose most subtle contributor was the Italian Marxist Antonio Gramsci has focused attention on the ideological dimension of social conflict and the capacity of subordinate-class consent to forestall movements from below.

Gramsci's views stand in contrast to a remarkably undialectical version offered by Marx and Engels, who wrote that "the ideas of the ruling class are in every epoch the ruling ideas. . . . The class which has the means of material production at its disposal, has control at the same time over the means of mental production, so that thereby, generally speaking, the ideas of those who lack the means of mental production are subject to it."[7]

Gramsci's formulation is more nuanced: a worker's consciousness is dual, "contradictory"; it contains one part "implicit in his activity and which truly unites him with all his fellow-workers in the practical transformation of the real world" and another, "superficially explicit or verbal, which he has inherited from the past and uncritically accepted."[8] The working class's own "conception of the world" expresses itself only occasionally; more commonly revealed is "a conception which is not its own but borrowed from another group," borrowed "for reasons of submission and intellectual subordination."[9]

However "superficially explicit or verbal," the part of workers' consciousness that is borrowed from dominant groups, which Gramsci frequently referred to as "common sense," is capable of blocking lower-class action. "This verbal conception is not without consequences," wrote Gramsci. "It binds together a specific social group, it influences moral conduct and the direction of will, in a manner more or less powerful, but often powerful enough to produce a situation in which the contradictory character of consciousness does not permit of any action, any decision or any choice, and produces a condition of moral and political passivity."[10] The power of dominant "conceptions of the world" to invade working-class consciousness and block action is one of the meanings Gramsci gave the term *hegemony*.[11] Many contemporary writers follow Gramsci in claiming that the operation of ideological hegemony contributes to social peace and that when subordinate groups move from quiescence to collective resistance, this shift may be sparked by a prior move away from intellectual subordination.[12]

Among the reasons why recent scholars have rejected ideological domination in favor of strategic interpretations of subaltern action are the very real methodological difficulties entailed in demonstrating hegemony at work. Consider Scott's notion of "public" and "hidden" transcripts. Even if the weak see through every effort of the powerful to mystify the nature and dynamics of social domination, they may still find it expedient to appeal "explicitly and verbally" to the principles of dominant ideology—not, à la Gramsci, because they have uncritically accepted this ideology but because it is in their strategic interests to do so. Scott offers the example of poor peasants cagily shaming the rich into extending charity to them by appealing to traditional Islamic and secular norms. The shame-driven concession of charity makes day-to-day life easier for the dominated even if it fails to permanently improve their material or social conditions; and no more deeply transformative line of action is realistically open to them. When the poor act in this way, they contribute "willy nilly to the public legitimacy" of the principles to which they "strategically appeal."[13] The "public transcript" will be full of such interactions. Because it is the public transcript that outside observers are most likely to "read," we will be led toward the false conclusion that the weak really believe the words they mouth and the practices they act out for purely strategic reasons. Another methodological difficulty arises from the fact that the weak do not habitually talk about social arrangements that are radically different from those they experience. But this may be true for reasons other than that they cannot under any circumstances imagine radically different arrangement or aspire to them.

The answers to five questions will help us determine whether hegemony, in the Gramscian sense outlined earlier, was at work in Peru.

1. Does lower-class culture replicate the discourse of the dominant? We must distinguish situations of cultural domination from ones in which subaltern groups avoid mobilization for strategic reasons (prior experience of failure, realistic appraisal of costs of mobilization, such as repression). The appropriate method here is content analysis of various genres or outlets of consciousness, such as verbal discourse, written texts, artistic works, and so forth. We should

also specify as precisely as possible the settings and mechanisms through which dominant ideas penetrate popular political culture.

2. If popular culture does indeed mirror dominant culture, do these shared beliefs, values, and visions of possible social worlds play a role in supporting the existing social order? We must distinguish between mere influence and a more thoroughgoing cultural domination. A shared taste for Mozart among musically cultivated wealthy and poor listeners is weak evidence of cultural domination; a shared belief in Horatio Alger–like social mobility in a highly static society is stronger evidence. We should also be alert to several discursive strategies that the dominant may deploy: The lower classes may learn that their plight is divinely ordained, natural, justified by a gulf separating them from the dominant in learning, cultivation, or technical skills. They may learn that their subordination is practically immutable,[14] better than any likely alternative, or good for them.[15] Or they may learn that the values and lifestyles of their social superiors are both attractive and not fundamentally different from their own; that is, there might be cultivated in them an affinity for, an identification with, the dominant.

3. Is the lower classes' apparent internalizing of dominant discourse, values, or sense of alternatives more than a pose? This might be labeled the "Scott test," because James Scott has so effectively made us aware that what looks like mental domination may be nothing more than the weak cagily appealing to the ideals of dominant ideology as a way of extracting some marginal material benefit.

How does one go about distinguishing between a calculated pose and a deeply felt belief? Scott suggests that it would be unwise to draw evidence from settings where the lowly actor is in the potentially constraining presence of his or her superiors, where we are likely to hear the poor dissimulating their belief in the "public transcript." The discourse of the slave is more reliable in the slave quarters than it is in the master's house; or the discourse of poor peasants is more reliable when their wealthy neighbors are absent. Another methodological device for distinguishing between deference as pose and deference as internalized domination is, not just to tap slices of attitudes and ideas, but to reconstruct, to the extent that this is possible, the fuller set of ideas and attitudes of subaltern groups, their worldview. Deference in someone who in other contexts is overwhelmingly class conscious, strategic, and assertive suggests posturing; deference in someone who is frequently admiring of the rich and powerful signifies a more deeply internalized cast of mind.

4. Does apparently consensual or accommodating outward behavior reflect the subordinate-class actor's realistic assessment that any other kind of behavior would bring on repression? A constant theme of writers arguing against hegemony is that repression, not consent, is at the core of social order. Outside analysts who find the demands of peasants or workers to be limited by the conservative terms of dominant ideology underestimate the power of remembered or anticipated repression: they ask subaltern actors to engage in acts of rebellion that would amount to suicide.

How do we know whether we are witnessing the effects of repression or of consent when we see subaltern actors apparently accommodating to an oppressive social order? The question raises methodological difficulties. There are good reasons not to expect subaltern actors to keep up a running account of the likelihood that various sorts of acts will lead to repression. A dull, constant level of intimidation may be so permanent a part of the landscape that subaltern actors are not fully conscious of its impact in constraining their own actions. People who have lived through civil wars attest to the psyche's tendency to downplay or "normalize" surrounding violence. And the most permanent parts of the landscape are the ones least commented on: the fish, as Gramsci wrote, do not talk about the water. Therefore it would be a mistake to conclude that if subaltern actors do not talk about repression it is not in fact limiting their actions.

A research strategy for dealing with this problem is to explore hegemony in places where accommodation and challenges to the surrounding order occur simultaneously, despite well-grounded fears of repression. If in these settings a set of accommodators have before them the example of a set of rebels, the case is less convincing that accommodators would do otherwise if repression did not threaten. Lower-class Lima in the recent period is, as we will see, exactly such a setting.

A second common criticism of the concept of intellectual subordination is that it serves the interests of intellectuals or parties voicing it and therefore is suspect in ways that more detached analyses are not. This criticism will be tempered to the extent that members of subaltern classes themselves describe the working of ideological domination. This suggests a another question:

5. In situations where the lower classes appear to have abandoned a mentality more deeply marked by dominant ideas and values, what is their understanding of how and why their way of looking at the world has changed? In addition to grounding analysis in the actor's own interpretation and understandings, and thus avoiding the condescension of the notion of "false consciousness," such evidence will strengthen the case against the view that apparently dominated ways of looking at the world are merely a pose.

The chapters that follow tell the story of the changing impact of state intervention in lower-class political life. Political culture was the mechanism of intervention. The state operated this mechanism relatively successfully in fostering a culture of consent for many decades. But under military rule in the 1970s, when the state shifted to a critical and mobilizing political culture, the mechanism became unwieldy. Poor city residents, mobilized under a cautious, vertically integrated structure, spilled over into movements that threatened the military leadership. Official slogans like "full participation" and "social mobilization," once they became lodged in the belief systems of the poor, inspired visions of alternative social and political arrangements that were anathema to the military government.

The state failed not only to control subaltern mentalities, however important this may have been, but also to provide effective organizational and, behind them, incentive structures. The Peruvian military government, in common with contemporary regimes in the region, had corporatist intentions.[16] It wished to sweep away the messy party system and replace it with a structure of interest representation in which singular, state-chartered, pyramidal organizations would channel "demands" (really information) upward and officials would channel resources downward. The favored organizations would be "popular"—the regime was progressive—and the system would be orderly.

The failure of this particular state corporatist project is of broad interest. Political theorists are searching for alternative political arrangements that promote equality and community in light of socialist failures in the East and foundering social democracy in the West. One model offered is a version of corporatism in which not just labor but a heterogeneous set of grassroots organizations, including community-development organizations, parent-teacher associations, and consumer groups, for example, are given greater power and resources in exchange for providing access to populations the state wishes to reach.[17] Just such a project failed brilliantly in Peru. That the context was a dependent capitalist country and that the failure was not entirely endogenous to the political model do not erase Peru's significance as an object lesson.

The Methods and the Field Site

On the right bank of the Rímac River, across the stone bridge from Lima's Plaza de Armas, lie the antique alleyways and narrow streets of Rímac, or "below the bridge," as older residents know this district. Despite the squalor of roadside garbage dumps and the huge gashes on the tarred surfaces of its neglected thoroughfares, Rímac retains a feeling of grandeur. It is possible to imagine its residents of the colonial era, many of them of African descent, the cobblers and carpenters who served the aristocratic mansions on the other side of the river.

But as one continues north, the historic air soon evaporates. Past a military garrison, past the proud if slightly dilapidated National Engineering University, a different kind of community spreads on each side of the Tupac Amaru Highway. Here all is new: the stark cement houses, hardware stores, and dingy restaurants that line the highway; the simpler dwellings lying on the hills rising up east of the highway, many nothing more than sheets of braided straw sewn to seams of dried cane; the trees, planted no more than ten years earlier. This particular set of shantytowns, or "young towns"—*pueblo joven* was the euphemistic term Peru's military government used in the 1970s to replace the denigrating *barriada*—forms the submunicipal district of Independencia,[18] where 160,000 factory workers, washerwomen, street vendors, sweatshop hands, and myriad other poor people and their children live. The scene is the same in any one of hundreds of communities housing Lima's poor. Indeed, in its youth (the earliest of Independencia's shantytowns appeared in 1960) and its verticality (it spreads upward into sandy hills), Independencia is more typical of Lima's poor districts than are the antique slums of Rímac.

In 1985 and 1986 I turned to Independencia to try to understand the changing political life of Peru's urban poor. My choice of Independencia combined design and circumstance. A preliminary sounding of several working-class neighborhoods allowed me to exclude some as atypical. Lima's older working-class districts, such as Rímac and La Victoria, house a smaller population and have less of a separate identity than does the typical "young town." The "young towns" are located farther from central Lima, are more socially homogeneous and more thoroughly residential, and in general represent a spatially autonomous lower-class district. I eliminated as a possible site for research Villa El Salvador, a large lower-class district located south of the city. Although fascinating, Villa El Salvador is atypical of Lima's newer lower-class districts in that it was formed all at once in a single, well-organized land invasion. I sought instead a district that was built up gradually through a combination of land invasions and government housing programs, a more typical pattern.

In the districts that met these requirements access was an important factor in my decision where to work. In the context of growing popular mobilization and still mild but psychologically intimidating police and military repression, there were compelling reasons to begin research in a working-class district that opened the doors of its political life to me. Independencia, where a young female mayor presided over the municipal government, was such a district.[19]

I made daily visits to Independencia between early 1985 and mid-1986.[20] The first year or so was devoted to developing a working relationship with officials and staff in the municipal administration, especially in the Office of Neighborhood Participation, established by the United Left municipal administration in 1983 and charged with furthering community activism and overseeing relations between community groups and the mayor's office. In this early phase I also gained a knowledge of Independencia's grassroots organizations, including neighborhood associations, "popular dining halls" (collectively run soup kitchens where members prepared and distributed heavily subsidized meals to their members), church and women's clubs, youth groups, and many more. I made return visits to the district in 1988, 1989, 1990, 1992, and 1993.

The material presented in this study reflects my knowledge of and participant-observation in several of these organizations. It also draws on extensive taped interviews with two dozen community leaders, activists, and residents, some more involved than others in community life. In carrying out the more formalized, taped interviews, I typically returned for at least one repeat interview, and in some cases I returned three or four times. Some of the many hours of taped interviews were transcribed by a Peruvian college student for closer analysis while the fieldwork was under way. In these cases I was able to follow up on fertile lines of questioning in repeat interviews with the same person. All of the interviews were eventually transcribed. The latter part of my fieldwork was taken up in conducting a large sample survey of Independencia's voters, which I report on in chapter 6. This second stage of my research did not signal the end of participant-observation, because the survey itself became a kind of community activity, with the members of two local youth organizations recruited as paid interviewers.

Outline of the Study

The chapters that follow discern a developmental, causal sequence linking the state with the poor by undertaking empirical analysis at three levels: (1) analysis of the nature and (largely unanticipated) consequences of the strategic programs of the military regime; (2) analysis of the resulting dualism of accommodating versus confrontational belief systems or mentalities I found among community leaders and the general population of Independencia; and (3) analysis of the parallel dualism of systems of action I found in the community organizations of Independencia.

Part 1, "The State and Social Movements," operates at the first level. Chapter 2 explores the political life and culture of the popular sectors from the oligarchic state period of the 1930s through the late 1960s. Chapter 3 explores the transformation of lower-class political life during the period of military rule in the seventies. Chapter 4 analyzes how these movements of the urban poor persisted under renewed civilian rule in the eighties and early nineties, without fully displacing a "clientelist" pattern of accommodation. The focus of these three chapters is on the institutional and political changes the urban poor underwent as they interacted with a changing state and political system.

Part 2, "Social Movements and Political Culture," operates at the second and third levels of empirical analysis, discerning historically produced dualisms in local systems of mentalities and action. Chapter 5 provides a fine-grained analysis of the political action and world-views of Independencia's inhabitants. The chapter reveals a bifurcated local political culture reflecting the shift to a movement politics along with the survival of clientelism. Chapter 6 draws on survey data to explore the bifurcated mentalities and practices associated with local political culture among Independencia's mass voting population. Chapter 7 returns to the theoretical issues taken up at the outset of the study: the successes and limitations of clientelism and state-sponsored systems of lower-class interest representation and the usefulness of the concept of hegemony or intellectual domination for understanding the suppression of a movement politics in some periods and its emergence in others.

Chapter Two

The Lower Classes
under the Oligarchic State

Before analyzing the impact of military-corporatist rule on the urban poor, it will be useful to examine the preceding period, known to Peruvian historiography as that of the *oligarchic state,* which lasted from the early 1930s to the late 1960s.[1] In this chapter I will argue that, despite the rise in the early 1930s of political parties interested in promoting labor unionism and in mobilizing working-class voters, these parties had only a small impact on poor urban neighborhoods. Organizations in the neighborhoods and their leaders remained enmeshed, instead, in clientelist networks. Clientelism stressed face-to-face ties with government officials (rather than membership in parties) and leadership centralized in a small group among a broader population that only became mobilized for very limited purposes.[2] Clientelism both rested on and in turn encouraged a political culture in which strains of deference and fatalism coexisted with upper-class affinity: a tendency for poor people to admire the values and lifestyles of the elite and to see themselves as sharing these values and lifestyles.[3] This popular culture also put considerable faith in the idea that national "progress" would inevitably and automatically lift the poor out of poverty.

Clientelism and the Oligarchic State

*When I go see someone at the mayor's office or
at the* pueblos jovenes *office, I always want to*

be able to tell them that our community doesn't
cause trouble.
> Shantytown leader, quoted in Dietz,
> "Bureaucratic Demand-Making and
> Clientelistic Participation"

Until the 1970s poor people in Peru's cities would follow certain implied rules of behavior in approaching government officials and other powerful actors. They would cultivate ties with one or two individuals in the relevant government agency or ministry, and they would retain those ties until their task was completed or until they gave up on ever completing it. Their outward attitude was one of deference and politeness; they would try to coax the individual official or bureaucrat to concede assistance, which was seen as an extension of personal charity. In return for whatever aid the poor community received, its leaders would make a public display of gratitude, commemorating the charitable act in a ceremony or perhaps naming a school, street, or building after their benefactor. These halting, limited, and ad hoc efforts largely described the Peruvian state's relationship with the urban poor.[4]

This clientelist pattern might have been eroded by political parties seeking a class-conscious mobilization of workers. But neither of the working-class-oriented parties emerging from the crisis years of the Great Depression—the populist APRA and the Communist Party— eroded clientelism.[5] The Peruvian Communist Party, founded by the socialist intellectual José Carlos Mariátegui in 1929 as the Peruvian Socialist Party, foundered after his early death in 1930. Repression and strategic errors by the party relegated it to a position of little importance in Peruvian politics until it revived under the peculiar circumstances of military rule in the late 1960s (see chapter 3).

From the 1930s through the 1950s APRA did create militant labor unions and cultivate a loyal segment of the lower-class electorate. But APRA did not manage to intervene in the clientelist relationship between poor neighborhoods and the oligarchic state. The reasons for this failure are complex. APRA was a populist party founded in 1928. Its founder, Victor Raúl Haya de la Torre, stressed a revolutionary alliance of workers and the middle class, in contrast to Mariátegui's "broad front" of workers and peasants. In its first two decades APRA consolidated loyal support among unionized workers, particularly in the north of the country, and this constituency of working-class *apristas* repeatedly pressed the party toward revolutionary action, for example, in revolts carried out in 1932 and 1948. On the other hand, APRA's leadership, and the ideology of *aprismo* fashioned by Haya de la Torre, contained features of both strident workerism and deference toward technically and educationally superior "professionals." In the mid-fifties, when Peru was emerging from an eight-year military dictatorship under the rightist regime of General Manuel Odría (1948–56), APRA's leadership accepted a compromise with civilian politicians in which APRA regained legal status in return for restraining more militant labor leaders associated with the party, particularly in the north. This period of "cohabitation" created schisms in the party and signaled the beginning of its turn away from social demands that it had earlier advanced; significant, for example, was the opposition of APRA's parliamentary group to land reform proposals in the mid-sixties.

For different reasons, then, neither of Peru's lower-class-oriented political parties was available to encourage mass defection from the politics of clientelism among the organizations growing out of the poor residential communities in the middle decades of the twentieth century.[6] The absence of such a mobilizing party left these communities to develop relations with state bureaucrats and sometimes with conservative political leaders (such as Odría). The combination of weak worker-oriented political parties, clientelist popular sectors, and a highly conservative state had a more than incidental impact on Peru's pattern of national development, including economic development. One would be hard-pressed to find a South American country more devoted than Peru to open-market economic policies in the mid-twentieth century, when most South American states pursued strategies of import-substitution industrialization.[7]

Cultural Dimensions of Clientelism under the Oligarchic State

Those who have studied popular political culture in the period of the oligarchic state have uncovered attitudes and mentalities that reflect a dominant discourse concerned with justifying sharp social hierarchies, what Steve Stein has called a "political culture of mass dependence."[8] Stein and others point toward the schools, both public and church-run, as settings where this discourse was purveyed. Gonzalo Portocarrero and Patricia Oliart have engaged in a painstaking review of school textbooks through much of Peru's republican history.[9] They found that twentieth-century textbooks contained more rigid and approving messages concerning the class structure than did nineteenth-century textbooks. According to Portocarrero and Oliart, the nineteenth-century liberal elites who proclaimed the potential equality of Indians and Peruvians of European descent were freer to do so because their writings would reach only the latter. When public education was extended to the urban poor and the peasantry in the first decades of the twentieth century, such notions of underlying equality gave way to greater respect for inequalities. That Peru's schools became places where children from the families of artisans and workers were encouraged to accept their inherited position of subordination was not lost on critics of the day: one called the schools "small barracks where the working class youth shrivels up."[10]

Working-class students were trained well into the 1960s, for example, in a discipline known as "urbanity" *(urbanidad),* or etiquette. The most widely used manual of urbanity included instructions evoking a caste system, such as that when social "inferiors" passed "superiors" on the street the former should step aside: "Urbanity greatly respects those categories established by nature, by society and by God himself, and therefore it obligates us to give preferential treatment to some people over others, according to their age, their social position, their rank, their authority and their character."[11]

The Peruvian Catholic Church was highly conservative and closely bound to large agricultural interests well into the twentieth century. In classrooms and masses and through its vast influence upon the society at large, church officials echoed the support for hierarchy that was promulgated in public schools. Thus in a 1937 pastoral letter, the archbishop of Lima urged the view that "poverty is the most certain path toward human happiness. Only the State that triumphs in making the poor appreciate the spiritual treasures of poverty can resolve its social problems."[12]

Antonio Gramsci, writing from his prison cell, despaired of writing a history of "common sense, impossible to reconstruct for lack of documentary material."[13] But social historians have used tools such as oral history and the interpretation of the artifacts of popular culture to reconstruct this culture. Among the historians of Peru, Stein has pursued this line of research farthest in the urban setting.[14] He has closely analyzed the lyrics of creole waltzes, a working-class musical style that first appeared at the turn of the century and became immensely popular in the 1930s. He concludes that "resignation as a response to adversity and crisis, fatalistic acceptance of bad luck, and deference toward—combined with dependence on—'superior' figures, emerged as primary values of the popular masses from the lyrics of creole waltzes."[15] Typical are the lyrics of one waltz that exclaimed:

> I don't want luck, I don't want it,
> With my bad luck I'm content,
> To rise up and then fall,
> Is a greater torment.[16]

The internalizing of messages encouraging passivity was aided by the ambivalent impact of *aprismo,* by far the most powerful cultural force among the more politicized sectors of Peru's working classes for several decades after the Depression. Haya de la Torre and APRA did cut across the traditional grain in emphasizing to workers their collective ability, through APRA, to improve the material conditions of their lives; in this sense *aprismo* stressed lower-class solidarity and the potential effectiveness of working-class action. But against these themes, APRA ideology also contained themes of deference toward professionals and technocrats and a premise of worker's inferiority in the skills necessary for national leadership. This latter current was consistent with APRA's program of achieving change by allying workers with the middle classes.

That *aprismo* reinforced a certain deference among workers toward their middle-class allies is reflected in the words of Arturo Sabroso, an *aprista* and textile union leader:

A government totally made up of people from the proletariat was never considered as a possibility. Precisely when we became convinced of this some fellow workers said, fine, we will join the Party, but fifty percent workers and fifty percent intellectuals in everything: deputies, senators, everything. Others of us reasoned that no, impossible to have half workers. In a parliamentary block you have to have professional men, technicians, doctors, engineers, economists, lawyers, professors, workers and employees. For study and consultation on many problems you need experts in their fields. This will assure that all the studies can be more effectively carried out.[17]

The technocratic requirements of governing meant that APRA's working-class constituency ought not to seek direct parliamentary representation, not even to the extent of constituting half of the party's parliamentary bloc.

It is also noteworthy that early in APRA's existence the deference that Sabroso counseled was controversial. APRA responded to and probably encouraged a strain in working-class political culture that aspired toward workers' more direct control over "their" political party, and through this control a more direct access to state power (through mechanisms such as the one Sabroso and his coworkers were debating, parliamentary representation). The very presence of this contrary position argues against seeing the dominant discourse of the oligarchic state period as having had complete success in penetrating working-class culture at all levels. Still, Sabroso's contrary position of deference to professionals with greater technical skills echoed that of Haya de la Torre and most of APRA's high leadership. This became the prevailing position within the party. Thus, according to Stein and others, the overall impact of APRA was to reinforce elements in working-class political culture purveyed by the oligarchic state and to smother opposing and more militantly workerist strains.

Voting behavior provides additional evidence of the influence of hegemonic political culture among the lower classes. Available evidence indicates that in the period between the 1930s and the 1960s the voting patterns of Lima's lower classes differed little from those of the city's wealthy and middle-class residents. Stein, who has investigated the 1931 presidential elections closely, claims that the loss of APRA's Haya de la Torre in those elections reflected the support of many lower-class voters for Luis M. Sánchez Cerro, the military lieutenant colonel who also was the favored candidate of the economic elite.[18] Analysis of voting behavior during the 1960s indicates that these same patterns persisted three decades later, at the close of the oligarchic state period. Sandra Powell has shown that in the 1960s, voters in Lima's working-class districts supported candidates from reform-oriented, centrist, and conservative parties in substantially the same proportion as did voters in middle- and upper-class districts.[19] Henry Dietz modified these findings somewhat, using more sophisticated measures of socioeconomic status.[20] Dietz corroborates many of Powell's conclusions, such as that no party in the sixties relied primarily on the lower classes for support. Dietz does show that in the 1963 elections voting behavior was associated with socioeconomic status at the district level. But even that year the pattern was much weaker than the one that would emerge as a regular feature of elections after 1980 (see chapter 4).

The ideological tenor of the parties that low-income voters supported also suggests the absence of a class-conscious popular political culture. Thus in the 1963 presidential elections, 36 percent of low-income districts supported the former military dictator Manuel Odría, 39 percent supported the mildly reformist Popular Action, and only 24 percent supported the traditionally worker-oriented APRA.[21] Odría and his wife gave out gifts of clothing and trinkets in lower-class neighborhoods, consciously copying the style of Juan and Evita Perón (but without Perón's interest in developing the labor movement).

In sum, for reasons connected with both the institutional and the cultural setting, urban lower-class politics in the oligarchic state period was the politics of clientelism. A small lower-class leadership sought individual assistance through personal ties to bureaucrats or political leaders, ties that facilitated a slow, grudging extension of specific material benefits in exchange for support or at least for good behavior. This is not to say that some workers never went beyond the bounds of clientelist practices or that some members of the popular sectors never found new strategies or unorthodox settings in which to voice unconventional demands. Poor people in Peru's cities who needed cheap housing, to take an example of great relevance to the present study, might through unconventional and disruptive action attract the attention of political leaders or religious authorities. They might even manage to achieve some of their goals. But they were unlikely to sustain momentum, focus attention on their plight for long, forge connections with others not directly involved in their local

TABLE 1. Lima Residents Living
in Shantytowns

Year	Population in Shantytowns (%)
1956	10
1961	17
1970	26
1982	33
1984	36

SOURCES: Alfred Stepan, *The State and Society: Peru in Comparative Perspective* (Princeton: Princeton University Press, 1978); and José Matos Mar, *Crisis del estado y desborde popular,* 2d ed. (Lima: Instituto de Estudios Peruanos, 1986).

concerns, or use one victory to press further demands. Events failed to become movements. And because poor people tended not to think of themselves as full rights-bearing citizens, much less consider a certain equality of life conditions as something a state ought to guarantee—ideas that their later counterparts did entertain—they tended to conceive of efforts to get land for housing or improve the physical setting of their communities as efforts to elicit charitable support from patrons.

Squatters and the Oligarchic State

The barriers to a more mobilizational politics during the oligarchic state period are illustrated by the squatter phenomenon. The problem of housing the urban poor became increasingly acute in the 1950s and thereafter, when a series of factors—the crisis of small-scale agriculture, a quickening of industrialization in the cities (particularly Lima), and hence a larger gap between urban and rural wages—combined to produce a surge in rural-to-urban migration (see table 1). Although migrants could improve their standard of living by moving to the cities, the vast majority came to the cities poor and, within the urban context, remained so.[22] This surge in the size of the urban popular sectors, in addition to the disinterest of the state or private actors in investing in low-income housing, lay behind the housing dilemma facing Peru's urban poor.

The squatter drive, or "land invasion," was a response to this dilemma.[23] In the capital city the wave of land drives that began in the fifties and continued in the nineties was prefigured by similar movements on a smaller scale earlier in the century. By the 1960s unoccupied lands relatively close to central Lima had become saturated, and squatters began to carve out communities ever farther from the colonial center. Government-owned barren hills, privately owned farmland, and empty tracts held by speculators all fell prey to squatters.[24] The main axis of this expansion ran northward and southward, paralleling the major transportation routes feeding the city: the "northern cone" arose around and between the northern segment of the Panamerican Highway and the Tupac Amaru Highway, while the "southern cone" spread around the southern Panamerican and Atocongo highways. Gaps in and between older industrial districts such as Ate, Vitarte, and Lurigancho, along the Central Highway, created the "eastern cone" districts, while squatters continued to appear in any unoccupied lands to the west, in Callao, even into the nineties.

Did land drives not represent a kind of movement politics, fed, perhaps, by a confrontational mentality among the urban poor in the oligarchic state period? One ought not to underestimate the physical dangers involved in squatting or the audacity of squatters who were breaking fundamental rules in a highly elitist society. They did so, furthermore, without being shielded by national political parties; although there is evidence of *aprista* support for some land invasions, there is also evidence that most invasion organizers were not connected with APRA and that APRA even blocked some drives.[25] But the audacity of this rule-breaking notwithstanding, land invasions were carried out with limited objectives and never threatened the broader social or political order.

For squatters themselves, land invasions during the fifties and sixties responded to a complex set of motivations and held a mixture of meanings. Much of the literature on the attitudes of squatters in Peru during this period is consistent with the corresponding literature from other Latin American countries.[26] It found squatters, particularly those who were highland migrants, to be confident of making upward social progress and interested in promoting the education and thus future employment and income prospects of their children (and sometimes of other young kin). Squatters saw themselves as already having progressed by leaving the countryside, and they were willing to accept hardships because of their confidence in their and their children's long-term advancement. Susan Lobo writes of a conversation among women in Ciudadela Chalaca, a lower-class community in the port city of Callao, that illustrates this sense of progress: "One woman grumbled at the bother involved in waiting her turn for use of the communal spigot. A number of the other women present adamantly protested, reminding her that in the highlands one must often walk long distances and carry water over steep terrain, while here in the city one only needs to step outside the door and wait."[27] Squatters who saw themselves as climbing a ladder of progress that had already carried them from the harsh countryside to the city saw land drives as just another rung on that ladder.

This confidence in progress is different from the more pessimistic fatalism that Stein found pervasive in working-class culture in the 1930s. But what the two have in common is the absence of an orientation toward seeking material or other benefits by making demands on the political system. A faith in inertial progress makes such demands unnecessary; fatalism makes them futile. Furthermore, the literature on squatters' motivations and mentalities suggests that they, like workers in the earlier period, would have seen making such demands as violating norms of decorum. Fatalism, passive faith in progress, and decorum are all very different from the mentality that would arise later among Lima's urban poor, according to which the government had an obligation to provide housing, running water, and other urban amenities to its poor, but nevertheless tax-paying, citizens. This attitude was suggested by Rosario Huayta's views toward health care that we glimpsed in chapter 1, and it will be explored more fully in chapter 5.

The unthreatening quality of land drives helps explain the state's ambivalence toward them. On the one hand, regimes such as General Odría's or the civilian governments of Manuel Prado in his second term (1956–62) and Fernando Belaúnde in his first term (1963–1968) were sensitive to landowners' and urban developers' indignant calls for the defense of private property, and rarely did a squatter invasion fail to provoke at least an effort at eviction. On the other hand, from the government's perspective squatter settlements provided an inexpensive solution to the problem of lower-class housing, requiring little public investment. Hence David Collier's finding that conservative leaders such as Odría actually encouraged land invasions. Conservative policymakers tried to cultivate an ideology of squatter "self-help": squatters should be granted small plots if they could prove through hard work and initiative that they deserved to be homeowners.

Pedro Beltrán, the director of president Prado's Commission for Agrarian and Housing Reform (CRAV), championed home ownership for the urban poor as a remedy for many ills. As a CRAV document produced in 1956 under Beltrán's directorship put it, home ownership "not only strengthens the moral fiber of family members and promotes self-fulfillment, but it also facilitates emotional stability, augments work productivity, reduces social conflict and delinquency, all of which translates into security and stability for the country and an increase in national productivity."[28]

The Peruvian state's response to squatter drives and the motivations behind those drives both point toward their relatively nonpolitical and unthreatening quality. Still, it is hard to believe that the government's initial response—police eviction efforts, which frequently left squatters injured—did not create disturbances in the prevailing views of the state as benevolent and progress as inevitable. In some residents' accounts of the land drives in Independencia I found a lingering sense of having been discriminated against by an elitist government and of having had to struggle too hard to achieve ends that came easily to residents of better-off communities. But the prevailing elite discourse emphasizing government benevolence and social harmony coming out of home ownership, along with a popular discourse emphasizing these same values as well as the inevitability of progress, gave squatters a limited language in terms of which to make sense of their experience, which in fact was harsh. Their experience of squatting and later struggles, experiences that exposed them to physical repression, frustrating delays, and disinterest on the part of the authorities, were not fully compatible with the dominant discourse on state-squatter ties. But they nevertheless echoed this

discourse and at some level believed in it. This gap between hegemonic discourse and experience would give resonance, in a very
changed context of military rule, to alternative understandings among
the poor of the political world in which they lived.

Action without Movement: Independencia, 1960

At midnight on November 18, 1960, dozens of trucks rolled up the
Canta road, north from Lima.[29] The caravan passed through several
miles of agricultural land before turning off the road at the flat stretch
known as the Pampa de Cueva, part of the Aliaga hacienda. There,
among the fields, some of them fallow, others planted with cotton,
corn, and sweet potatoes, five hundred families descended from their
trucks and started erecting huts from cane poles and straw mats. They
carefully selected fields lying fallow for the site of their land invasion.
By dawn the squatters had erected their temporary homes and were
trying to give the impression of routine daily life. A newspaper reporter on the scene reported that "hundreds of straw houses had been
raised, and the teacher Edmundo Aramburú was giving classes to
numerous youths."[30] This and other strategies had been painstakingly
discussed for months by members of the Pampa de Cueva Housing
Association, a group of residents of an older working-class district who
had initiated plans to occupy these lands.

The appearance of calm normality soon evaporated as dozens of
mounted police began the "dislodging" (*desalojo*), or eviction, of
the squatters. The Pampa de Cueva Housing Association had hoped
that the fact that much of the Pampa lay fallow would keep the police
at bay. The Pampa de Cueva and other areas had been named in a
1955 government decree as unused land subject to government ap-
propriation. But the Aliaga hacienda, which contained part of the
Pampa, was owned by the Nicolini family, powerful industrialists and
landowners; the authorities quickly responded when the dismayed
hacienda owner, Adela Iglesias de Nicolini, appealed to them for
assistance.

At 10:00 A.M. mounted police formed a phalanx at the edge of the
Canta road, west of the squatters; the cavalry was joined by regular
Civil Guardsmen and, eventually, a detachment of the Republican

Guard. A newspaper reporter observing the scene was affected by what turned into a violent confrontation: "The people, carrying flags and shouting 'Viva Peru,' took refuge in the nearby hills, and the cavalry turned in that direction, dispersing those who resisted them. The invaders ran away again, and again they were pursued. Mothers tried to shield their children from the horses, but inevitably there were injuries."[31] Some squatters responded by hurling stones; one policeman and several squatters were wounded.

Despite the violence of the attempted eviction, the authorities soon entered into negotiations with the squatters, negotiations that eventually turned in the squatters' favor. Press reports focused much attention on the land invasion; two APRA legislators visited the site; and two Communist Party lawyers offered advice. Squatter representatives were first granted meetings with President Prado and Peru's archbishop, the latter of whom reminded the squatters of the sanctity of private property, and later with officials from the ministry of justice.[32] After some false starts—at one point an official suggested that the squatters receive land grants in the Peruvian Amazon[33]—it was agreed that they would remain on the land and would contribute to compensating the Nicolini family, while the state would retain ownership. The new residents named their community Independencia.

The need to maintain an internal organization with authority over community affairs was made clear by the exigencies of daily life in the new settlement. Independencia's squatters had placed themselves, for a time at least, in a liminal zone, not quite part of the broader political society. Therefore they could scarcely call on the police to impose order among their members or to defend them against a variety of threats from the outside. A common problem was the appearance of newcomers, people who had not taken part in planning or carrying out the invasion but who hoped in the weeks after it had taken place to stake a claim to a small parcel. A second problem was crime among squatters, such as the theft of household goods from unguarded shacks, or violent arguments over where one family's plot ended and another's began. In addition to these and other internal problems, squatters never knew when the police might arrive and try to force them off the land.

The nagging problem of threatened eviction continued to color the memory of the land invasions of residents I interviewed a quarter-century later. A woman who squatted with others on a rocky hillside above the Pampa de Cueva in 1967 remembered repeated visits and threats by "Señorita Gloria," a housing ministry official. In one interview she recalled: "I finally said to her, 'We're Peruvians too, we have a right to this place.'" The invoking of national identity to justify holding land was consistent with the common practice of choosing election days and national holidays to invade lands and placing flags on squatters' shacks. It would not be a large step from these practices to the idea that poor people, as citizens, hold certain rights that they could demand of the state; and the link between this idea and the more strident demand-making of the kind that would become common later is not difficult to perceive. On the other hand, this woman (and many others) seemed to have thought of their adversaries, not as an institution, a government, or a state, but rather as individual people out to thwart them. It was Señorita Gloria, rather than the housing ministry or the Belaúnde government, who wanted to expel these squatters from the land.

Housing associations similar to those that organized the Pampa de Cueva land invasion were the organizational backbone of the new settlements. Aside from enforcing rules and protecting the settlements from outsiders, these early associations began the long and still unfinished task of shaping rocky, jagged, sloping, and completely unserviced tracts into liveable urban communities. Paths had to be cleared and straightened, and later they would be broadened and leveled. Only an exceptional few were to be paved—in Independencia not until twenty-five years after the original squatters' drive. Individual lots, grabbed up and staked out in the dead of night, had to be standardized in size, provoking endless disputes. For invaders, and even for inhabitants of the planned communities (such as Tawantin-suyu, a section of Independencia that grew out of a Belaúnde-era housing program), running water and electricity were distant dreams in the sixties.

To the extent that Independencia did over the years begin to resemble a stable, urban lower-class community, this was the result of the efforts of community members, and especially the housing associations that continued to form the core of the community's organizational life. From the perspective of later years, what is remarkable about these efforts of the 1960s is the degree to which the squatters' associations remained independent of political parties, the church, or other outside agents or institutions. Instead of having ongoing links with such outsiders, these associations typically approached lower- or middle-level government bureaucrats to request aid for specific community-improvement projects. Community leaders saw these ties as ones between individual officials and their communities; they did not try to institutionalize them, nor did they generally conceive of the aid they received as more than charitable assistance.

The link between Las Flores, a neighborhood in the hills above Independencia, formed by squatters in 1967, and a housing ministry engineer named Fernández was characteristic of this sort of relationship. The leaders of Las Flores's housing association approached Fernández, a middle-level government employee, for help in leveling the neighborhood's roads. Out of gratitude for the maps of the community's streets that Fernández produced, community leaders named the neighborhood's main street Calle Fernández. Leaders from this period expressed continuing gratitude to this beneficent individual; they never expressed the view that Fernández was a government employee providing a professional service that the community had a right to expect.

If government-squatter ties evolved in a context of individualized clientelism or quasi charity, ties between political parties and squatters in Independencia were rare throughout the 1960s. When individual politicians did attempt to cultivate a support base, their efforts generally amounted to no more than occasional campaign visits. APRA and the much smaller Communist Party might have been expected to have the closest ties with this lower-class community, but interviews in Independencia confirm the lack of interest among parties in shantytown residents (as opposed to unionizable workers). My interviews and research occasionally turned up *apristas* who had played roles in land invasions or later community affairs, but their party affiliation had been established in unions and they were given no encouragement to organize as party members in their barrios. Only later, after the Peruvian military government broadened the understanding of political communities to include residential communities of the urban poor, did the politicization of these communities begin.

Chapter Three

Military Rule
and the Transformation
of Lower-Class Politics

On October 3, 1968, a group of military officers ousted Peru's civilian president Fernando Belaúnde Terry, initiating one of the most unusual experiences of military rule in Latin American history.[1] Among the surprising outcomes of the period of military rule was the emergence of a mobilized, strident, rights-conscious segment of the country's shantytown population and thus a challenge to the previously dominant politics of clientelism.

The coup came because a reformist faction of the military saw the country's political parties and civilian leaders as incapable of carrying out reforms that it believed were urgently needed. From the outset the motivation for military takeover in Peru differed from that of other contemporary military takeovers in South America, where coups were a response to the perception of great economic disorder threatening elite interests and to a challenge from the Left. Although there was some element of this response in Peru, the self-declared Revolutionary Government of the Armed Forces saw its task as breaking the stranglehold of the traditional oligarchy and instituting a dynamic, redistributive form of economic development in which domestic private capital and state capital would play a larger role than foreign capital. Or, more accurately, an initially dominant part of the military leadership saw its task in this way; other military leaders, however, who would reassert themselves later in the 1970s, had goals similar to those of contemporary military regimes elsewhere in the region.[2]

The regime of Juan Velasco Alvarado has been interpreted as corporatist, or at least as aspiring to install an "inclusionary" corporatist-style system of interest representation.[3] This interpretation is accurate if we keep in mind the unorthodox qualities of this corporatist project and distinguish between the *effort* to install a corporatist structure and the *success* of such an effort. The Velasco experience illustrates the difficulty that inclusionary corporatists face in creating ties with the lower classes that move beyond clientelism, on the one hand, and in remaining in control of the mobilization they are likely to produce, on the other. It also illustrates the difficulty of constructing a corporatist system organized not around the labor movement but around residential communities of the poor. By transforming the political affiliation of the labor movement, by expanding educational opportunities open to the poor, by reorganizing and stimulating shantytown neighborhood organizations, and by imposing a far-reaching agrarian reform, the military regime under Velasco set off processes that would culminate in a new social movement among Peru's urban and rural poor.

Velasco and the Labor Movement

Among the most unusual outcomes of military rule in Peru was a strengthened labor movement. At the same time that contemporary South American military governments were abolishing unions and jailing or assassinating their leaders, the number of legally recognized unions doubled in Peru between 1968 and 1977, from 2,297 to 4,453. And as table 2 shows, the number of strikes per year was higher than during previous governments.[4] Successful regional and national strikes were also held, including a first, dramatic general strike in July 1977.

This strengthening of labor was a result of Velasco government policies as well as of factors beyond the government's control. Among the government's policies contributing to labor's growing strength was its Industrial Community program. Workers in certain industries were to share in the management and profits of the companies where they

TABLE 2.   Average Number of Strikes per Year
under Various Governments, 1956–1975

Regime	Average strikes/year
Prado (1956–62)	261
Pérez Godoy/Lindley (1962–63)	404
Belaúnde (1963–68)	397
Velasco (1968–75)	504

SOURCES: Isabel Yepes del Castillo and Jorge Bernedo Alvarez, *La sindicalización en el Perú* (Lima: Fundación Ebert and Pontificia Universidad Católica del Perú, 1985).

worked. Management found multiple ways of thwarting the Industrial Communities, such as by hiding profits and manipulating meetings in which workers took part. Workers who became involved in Industrial Communities and observed this maneuvering became dissatisfied with management and more rather than less militant. Union organizers took advantage of this growing dissatisfaction and used the Industrial Communities as organizational bases from which to attract workers. Thus Industrial Communities had the effect, unanticipated and unintended, of extending labor unions to new firms and industries.

The Velasco regime's changes in job security laws also contributed to the greater reach and militancy of labor unions. Among the obstacles facing the reformist military government was opposition from industrialists, who sabotaged reform efforts by reducing production and firing workers. The regime responded in 1970, implementing a job security law to end these mass firings; the move was also consistent with the prolabor stance of the regime's left wing. The new law stipulated that after a three-month trial period companies could fire workers only for a narrow set of reasons; firings could be appealed through the labor ministry and the courts. The measure deprived management of one of its most effective weapons in fighting union organizers, who were now relatively free to operate without fear of losing their jobs. Carmen Rosa Balbi notes that the new job security provisions and the Industrial Community together helped chip away at management's previously absolute disciplinary power within the factory.[5]

The Velasco military regime's capacity for making changes that would later return to haunt it was nowhere clearer than in its relations with labor federations.[6] The government's desire to construct a corporatist, nonpolitical (i.e., party-free) society required sapping the strength of APRA. This meant severing the tie between APRA and organized labor, since APRA was still the political party with the most resilient relationship with labor. Therefore, undermining the APRA-affiliated Confederation of Peruvian Workers (CTP) became a high priority for the Velasco regime. Toward this end in 1971 the government recognized the Communist Party-affiliated General Confederation of Workers of Peru (CGTP).

The unusual spectacle of a Latin American military regime lending support to a Communist Party-affiliated labor federation reflected the Party's support for this nationalist regime as well as the regime's drive to undermine APRA. The Communist Party was one of only a few political parties to declare itself in support of the regime (although it qualified its support as "critical"). The government's move was also intelligible given that Trotskyite, Maoist, Guevarist, and other New Left parties and guerrilla groups were still in the early 1970s insignificant political forces and unconnected both with the Communist Party and, for the most part, with the labor movement.[7] It was therefore difficult for the military government to see itself as contributing to strengthening the Marxist Left more generally, rather than simply weakening APRA by bolstering a friendly and relatively weak Communist Party. If a general leftward realignment of Peruvian society was already under way, this was not clear to military government strategists in the opening years of the 1970s.

But such a process *was* under way, and the Velasco regime's support of the CGTP unintentionally encouraged that process. By the end of the decade the CGTP had overtaken the CTP to become the largest labor confederation in Peru: 44 percent of all affiliated labor unions were affiliated with the CGTP. Furthermore, although the Communist Party retained control of the CGTP's leadership, many member unions that joined during the 1970s were organized by New Left parties, who were less friendly with the military rulers. In addition to helping create unions that would later join the CGTP, the new Marxist parties also sparked internal rebellions against an older APRA leadership in unions that subsequently shifted affiliation from the CTP to the CGTP.

The significance of these changes in labor's partisan affiliation and militancy went beyond the labor movement itself. The unionized labor force was a small segment of Peru's popular sectors. But unionized factory workers also tended to live in shantytowns and older urban ghettos. Henry Dietz's analysis of census data finds significant correlations between the blue-collar population and the squatter population of Lima's residential districts in the censuses of both 1961 and 1981.[8] Thus, much of Lima's industrial working class, which directly experienced the rise of the "classist" labor movement under military rule, lived in the same neighborhoods as the nonproletarian popular sectors. A certain spillover effect from the unions to the shantytowns was inevitable.

Velasco and the Shantytowns

The effects of the Velasco regime's policies on the political life of Peru's shantytowns were complex and contradictory.[9] The regime failed to achieve its desired goals of creating a more participatory yet loyal political base. On the one hand, the regime failed to root out, and indeed reinforced, clientelist forms of lower-class political practices. On the other hand, among segments of the shantytown population the regime unintentionally sparked an uncontrolled popular movement, one allied with various forces that would help bring down the military regime itself.

Several factors motivated the Velasco regime to orchestrate what it hoped would be a corporatist-style mobilization of the shantytowns of Lima and other cities. In contrast to earlier state leaders, Velasco and his advisers wished to transfer the Peruvian state away from its traditionally elite social base to the popular sectors. Its new social base, it hoped, would include a reorganized labor movement. But the fact that shantytown communities were unattached to APRA or to any other party made them tempting communities to cultivate.[10] In the end the Velasco regime's emphasis on organizing the popular sectors in the shantytowns helped broaden the definition of lower-class political communities from labor unions to residential communities.

To achieve its aims of improving the lives of the urban poor and attracting their loyalty, the government created new structures of local political activism. It implanted a pyramid of semirepresentative, neighborhood-based organizations. The bottom echelon of this new organizational structure was the block-level "neighborhood committee" *(comité vecinal)*, composed of heads of household of a given square block. Members of neighborhood committees elected delegates to central committees; these delegates in turn elected a Committee to Promote Development (Comité de Promoción y Desarrollo, or COPRODE). Neighborhood committees, which replaced independent housing associations, were involved in the distribution of land titles and general community-improvement projects; they also encouraged residents to attend community-development seminars and other government-sponsored events. The government's link with these new neighborhood associations was the National System to Support Social Mobilization, or SINAMOS, created in 1971 and charged with promoting popular participation throughout the country.[11] In remaking squatter associations and their links with the state the government's aims were, as Henry Dietz has noted, "simultaneously (and paradoxically) the encouragement and the control of local, autonomous decision-making."[12]

Dietz captures well the ambiguities of the Velasco regime's impact on the shantytowns, its mixture of revolutionary transformation and the reproduction of clientelism. Influential government officials like Carlos Delgado, a close Velasco adviser, wished to undertake "a historical process . . . to change the structure of power of [Peruvian] society"[13] and saw the neighborhood committees as empowering the popular sectors and thus contributing to this structural change. The vision of leaders like Delgado and the efforts of those implementing Velasco policies would produce a real mobilization of segments of the shantytown communities. But commitment to this kind of transformation at the highest levels of government was weak; this, in addition to a certain inertia at lower levels of the bureaucracy and among the squatters themselves, reinforced clientelism. It is worth quoting

Dietz's account of the microrelationship typical of *pobladores* and government employees at the Dirección de Pueblos Jóvenes (DPJ), the precursor to SINAMOS:

> [C]oming to the DPJ . . . the individual presents himself as retiring (in the sense of not being pushy or impatient), eager to listen and to please, and thankful for the opportunity of coming to the DPJ. . . . [The *poblador*'s] respect for authority stems from several sources and has several motives. Besides the fact that class and occupational differences create strongly felt and observed hierarchical perceptions, the presence (in some degree) of a patron-client relationship between the *poblador* and the DPJ personnel may be very real. Indeed, the DPJ itself may be perceived by the *poblador* as a patron, as an "individual" or source to which he can go for assistance. . . .[14]

The description, which might just as well be of government-squatter contacts at the height of the oligarchic state, hardly gives the impression of a revolutionary government set on empowering the popular sectors.

It is possible to judge the Velasco regime too harshly in focusing on its inability to play even the limited transformative role the military, or a faction in the military, set for itself. In the 1980s a certain revisionism began to appear in the literature on the Velasco period, a revisionism that acknowledged the areas in which the regime attained some success in transforming Peruvian society.[15] In its education policies the regime went well beyond trading material rewards for tame support by offering the popular sectors the means to critically assess and improve their own conditions of existence. Portocarrero and Oliart see these changes as giving rise to a "critical idea" of Peruvian history and current social problems, in stark contrast to the conservatism meted out in the schools of the oligarchic state period.[16] Still, these and other transformative changes notwithstanding, the tension between the *poblador*'s real experience of the state as reported by Dietz and the desire of officials like Carlos Delgado to restructure power relations is palpable.

At the same time that much of the state-shantytown link repeated clientelist patterns of the past, when the regime did succeed in sparking a new spirit of participation it was much less successful at retaining the loyalties of newly activated squatters. The regime's inability to make the great improvements in the physical quality of the shantytowns that its rhetoric promised contributed to this failure: it raised expectations that it failed to meet. Indeed there was no consensus within the military over shifting resources to the popular sectors; in fact the Velasco regime subsidized middle- and upper-class housing more heavily than it did lower-class housing.[17] What is more, the resources available to the regime shrank over time; the effect was to further open the gap between promises of material improvement for the poor and real achievements.[18]

A second factor contributing to the Velasco regime's failure to control the movements that it inspired was the appearance in the shantytowns of a new set of parties and religious agents that successfully competed with SINAMOS for *poblador* support. Principal among them were cadres from Marxist parties and socially oriented representatives of the Catholic Church. The years of military rule coincided with the growth of a series of new Marxist parties and with the gathering of force of liberation theology among clerics, nuns, and lay church workers.[19] When SINAMOS and the regime failed to live up to their own rhetoric, or when the mobilizing phase of the regime gave way in mid-1975 to a more conservative and authoritarian one, these alternative agents of mobilization were well located to take over the movement that the regime had halfheartedly conceived.[20]

Also contributing to the regime's inability to create a participatory but loyal social base was the fact that SINAMOS was not entering an organizational void. The shantytowns included many self-contained community organizations, and sometimes these competed among themselves for local ascendancy. In its corporatist effort the regime (embodied by SINAMOS) had to take sides in these local conflicts, shoring up one organization and undermining the rest. The favored organization was likely to suffer from excessive dependence on SINAMOS, a dependence that fostered clientelism, while the disfavored organizations produced unruly activists, embittered and disposed to oppose the regime. Thus the matter of creating a monopoly of representation proved difficult for the Velasco regime.

To summarize, the Velasco regime paradoxically reinforced clientelist relations in the shantytowns at the same time that it sparked social movements. The actions of the regime that stimulated a new social movement broadened the definition of political communities of the popular sectors beyond the industrial working class, where Peru's worker-oriented parties had traditionally focused their efforts. The regime's actions also failed to achieve a lasting control over those who were newly mobilized; unintentionally produced newly strengthened actors, such as the Communist Party, the New Left, and the Catholic Church, who would carry mobilization beyond the bounds set by the regime; and created a grassroots opposition in neighborhoods where some organizations lost out in the regime's corporatist effort to charter single representative associations.

Independencia under Velasco

Many residents of Independencia welcomed the appearance of agents of the Peruvian state other than the police in their previously neglected community. Fifty-six percent of respondents in my 1986 survey recalled the Velasco government as a good one, making it more popular than any subsequent government with the exception of the then newly installed García administration.[21] Some whom I interviewed remembered the Velasco regime as a sort of national call to attention, one that would infuse pride and order into their "young towns." Even a barracks-like order was better than the chaos and indolence of the "civilian way of life." As one man put it:

> To be a civilian is one thing, and to be a military person is something else. For example, if you live in a straw shack, with a dirt floor, your bed is nothing more than a cot, when you sweep the dust rises—that's what civilian life means. In contrast, military life is like if you went to live in a house with a cement floor, strong walls, everything's clean. Military life is straighter, stricter.

Q: You mean the government wanted the military life for everyone?

A: They wanted people to live more comfortably, to be more presentable. Just giving the slums the name "young towns" signified a structural change. Imagine if someone came from an embassy, maybe the Chinese embassy, and they said "Which is the young town—for example—Tawantinsuyu?" They would see all the straw shacks, dirty, clothes hanging out. The military government wanted everything to be more presentable. If a person goes to a social dance, he can't go with dirty clothes, the clothes might be old but they have to be clean.

This man was pleased with the military's attention and untroubled by the paternalism of SINAMOS, which "gave talks, like to children in a school." Many neighborhoods obligingly founded neighborhood committees, central committees, and COPRODEs; the "neighborhood committee" label remained prevalent even into the 1990s.

But the prevalence of the neighborhood committee label should not obscure the fact that among some segments of Independencia's population the Velasco regime raised expectations that it then failed to satisfy and stimulated an ethic of participation that it failed to limit. A source of disappointment in Independencia, in line with the response elsewhere, was the regime's failure to provide concrete benefits. The granting of titles to land is one example. Alfred Stepan has shown that the regime wanted to distribute titles legalizing squatters' tenure over their land as a nearly cost-free way of gaining support. But a 1985 survey showed that a decade after Velasco's fall from power, two-thirds of Independencia's families still lacked legal ownership of the land on which their homes stood.[22] During the Velasco period fifty-four barrios in Independencia gained legal status as communities, called "young towns" *(pueblos jovenes)*. But only a minority of families received individual title to the land on which their homes were built.

Some Independencia residents turned against the regime because of its failure to *rendir*, to follow through on its promises. But some turned against it immediately, not just when promises went unfulfilled. This was true in barrios where two or more associations already existed. Las Flores, where the district mothers' club was locked in a longstanding conflict with the housing association, was one such setting. The conflict in the early 1970s revolved around a building that the mothers' club proposed to construct with the help of church funds. The housing association leadership saw the building as a threat to its own preeminence in the neighborhood and said that if the mothers' club building were to go up, it would have to be open to the community at large and administered by the housing association. The mothers' club rejected these conditions, and the housing association blocked construction of the building. (The conflict was symptomatic of deeper ones, to be explored in greater depth in chapter 5.)

When SINAMOS arrived in Las Flores in 1972 it established a neighborhood committee by changing the name and statutes of the existing housing association; the old housing association leadership was reelected under new procedures and became the Las Flores Neighborhood Committee. For the mothers' club members the alliance between SINAMOS and the neighborhood committee alliance made SINAMOS an enemy. Julia Romero, a mothers' club activist from the period, remembered in our interviews the many ways that she and others sabotaged SINAMOS activities. When the SINAMOS organizer asked mothers' club members to attend the swearing-in of the new neighborhood committee leaders, the women did not refuse, but they did not attend. At a series of well-publicized SINAMOS-sponsored classes on fish processing, the club was again absent.

Romero's ongoing squabbles with SINAMOS illustrate the regime's tendency to create an opposition to itself in its efforts to impose a monopoly of representation in the shantytowns. Such a tendency affects corporatist regimes that scholars have called "inclusionary," ones that rely more heavily on incentives than on repression and exclusion in constructing a relationship between the corporatist state and society.[23] Inclusionary regimes are particularly vulnerable because of their need to disfavor some representative organizations without taking the further step of eliminating them. SINAMOS was not in the business of repression. Recalcitrants like Romero knew they risked little more than the withholding of favors from the government; they were unlikely to face jail or harsher sanctions. In fact the subsequent careers of several Las Flores Mothers' Club members show that SINAMOS unintentionally provided a sort of training program in community activism. People like Romero, who went on to become a prominent local activist admired by many as a tireless fighter, learned valuable lessons in strategy and confidence from taking on powerful political opponents, agents of the military state.

The Las Flores Neighborhood Committee, in contrast, which enjoyed SINAMOS backing, remained clientelist in both attitudes and practices.[24]

Other new arrivals in the shantytowns helped remake the texture of politics in Independencia during the Velasco era. Cadres from Marxist parties either acted clandestinely or came as students, researchers, or ostensibly nonpartisan neighborhood organizers. Some party cadres even came to Independencia as participants in regime-sponsored programs.[25] That the New Left, sneaking into the shantytowns under the nose of the military regime, contributed to a new movement politics is less than surprising. Almost all parties of the Left condemned the Velasco regime;[26] they had ideological and institutional motives for promoting social movements that would discredit it. The progressive church played the same role.[27]

But if the Left and the church, like the state itself, helped spark a movement politics in the shantytowns, did these new outside actors also—and again like the state—reinforce clientelist practices? My observations and interviews in Independencia produced examples of both mobilizing and clientelist ties between *pobladores* and these outside agents. The relationship that developed between Rosario Huayta, the Feminine Committee member introduced in chapter 1, and a woman college student who was a neighborhood organizer and leftist party cadre illustrates one kind of pattern, where the outside mobilizer helped the *poblador* develop skills that allowed her to become more effective as a community activist. In this way their relationship eliminated the originally stark disparities of power between the two and went beyond clientelism. Huayta described the relationship in this way:

Gloria Ríos [the party organizer] was a great person, very very audacious, a person who never was afraid of anyone, very decided. . . . Even though there was no electricity, she would be with us until eleven or twelve at night, even though she didn't live here. She went up the hills with us and with the priest and Mother Eva; we went together in a commission, in the dark, we walked as a chain, even during the rainy season because we had to go to the Neighborhood Committee assemblies—that was during the time of SINAMOS. We went to the assemblies to say that we wanted a medical post. Some people applauded us; others disagreed. Gloria said, "No, we can't let ourselves be defeated." She never ordered us anywhere, she always went in front. . . . She gave me a good education. Before I was shy and thought that what I was going to say would seem stupid to other people. She said, "No, you have to say what you feel." When we went to assemblies she would say,

"You, Rosario, you have to speak without notes, without anything, because you're a person who knows how to handle yourself. You have to say what you feel, not what I tell you."

But it is also clear that under different circumstances this kind of relationship could echo a more traditional clientelism, with the cadre providing rewards in return for their clients' supporting their organizations, without any larger change in power relations occurring. A more authoritarian middle-class student than Ríos could easily reinforce a kind of class subservience in people like Rosario Huayta; and Huayta's admiration for Ríos contained elements of awe for the willingness of Ríos, a child of privilege, to scale barrio hills in the rain. The Catholic Church had a similarly complex impact in Independencia. If its main impact was to help mobilize the community, I also found evidence of its creating and reinforcing bonds of clientelism.

Post-Corporatist Military Rule and Social Mobilization

Six years after the coup that brought Velasco to power, the regime's popular support was declining, the Velasco faction's hold over the military loosening. On February 5, 1975, during a police strike, a mob burned the offices of SINAMOS.[28] The offices were not restored; nor did General Francisco Morales Bermúdez, who six months later ousted Velasco from power, reconstruct Velasco's corporatist edifice. But the legacy of Velasco, his championing of participation while failing to define its limits, was soon to produce a level of social mobilization that would help bring an end to military rule itself. So intense was this mobilization that partisans of revolution saw the political moment as "prerevolutionary." But although no revolution occurred, the popular mobilization, because of its depth and extent, had a larger part in precipitating the transition to civilian rule in Peru than did such mobilization in most other South American countries.[29]

Some dimensions of the social mobilization of the Morales years are easier to demonstrate statistically than others. Several authors have documented the rise of labor mobilization. Evelyne Huber Stephens shows that strikes rose during both the Velasco and Morales regimes, with the number of workers involved reaching its peak in the final years of military rule. Nearly 1.4 million workers took part in strikes in 1978, a number almost ten times the average in the sixties and early seventies. "Strikes" also changed in nature. Some combined specific labor actions, protests over inflation and other general economic conditions, and movements to oust the military regime. The first national strikes in Peruvian history, in 1977, 1978, and 1979, were not so much strikes in a strict sense as coordinated mass protests in which union federations, students, shantytown organizations, peasant leagues, feminist groups, and others came together in coordinated action to voice a very broad set of demands.

The growth of unionism in this period also meant that unions appeared among sectors of the workforce that had previously been unorganized, most notably among public-sector employees and teachers. A new national teachers' union, the Unified Syndicate of Educational Workers of Peru (SUTEP), was founded in 1972.[30] The rise of SUTEP, which by 1978 had become the country's largest teacher's union, was particularly significant in that its political affiliation was with the Maoist Patria Roja (Red Fatherland) Party.[31] In this way public schools became a link between a formalized version of Marxist politics and working-class students. The SUTEP represented the flowing together of three streams of change initiated during the Velasco years: the surge in unionization, the strengthening of the Marxist Left, and the infusion of a "critical idea" of Peruvian society and history, as Portocarrero and Oliart have aptly put it, into school curricula.

In addition to easily documented changes, such as the growth of unions, and well-reported and sometimes spectacular events, such as national strikes, Peru's cities also saw a flurry of smaller street demonstrations involving *pobladores* from the shantytowns. Demonstrators demanded that their "young towns" be fitted with running water and electricity; they wanted garbage collection, police protection, health clinics, bus service, street paving, and parks. They also made less local demands, such as that prices for basic goods be brought down (and, by extension, that national economic policy take a different course). And on increasingly frequent occasions they demanded an end to military rule.

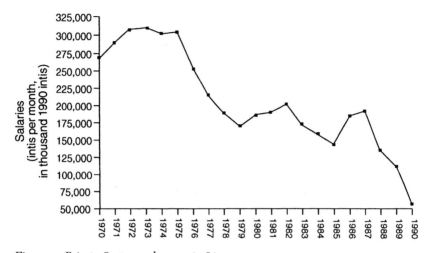

Figure 1. Private Sector real wages in Lima, 1970–1990.
SOURCE: Richard Webb and Graciela Fernández Baca de Valdez, *Perú en Números, 1991*. Lima: Cuánto S.A., 1991.

When neighborhood committees, women's clubs, youth groups, parish members, or even sports clubs from poor districts set up barricades to keep buses off the roads during the national strikes, their activities received much attention in the national press. But virtually lost to the written record are myriad marches, occupations and sit-ins at government ministries, open-air assemblies, hunger strikes, and other forms of pressure politics that flourished in the later years of military rule. In Independencia several moments crystallized the Morales years in the memories of residents. They recalled burning tires in the Tupac Amaru Highway to keep buses from operating during the national strikes; padlocking inside their schools teachers who ignored a SUTEP-organized teachers' strike; and campaigns to build health clinics and install services, campaigns involving loud marches before government buildings. Such activism was new in a country where popular urban politics had meant labor politics for many decades, indeed where poor neighborhoods had only recently come to be thought of as political communities.

A factor coming increasingly into play as a source of mobilization of unions, the urban poor, women, and others as military rule wore on was the dire state of the national economy. In 1973 the gross national product declined for the first time, and by 1975 the recession was eroding real incomes. The reasons for this downturn, which persisted into the 1990s with only two periods of respite, have been described well elsewhere.[32] What is clear is that in 1975 real salaries and wages were beginning a slide into a painfully long period of increased poverty for Peru's lower classes (see fig. 1).

It is undeniable that the deteriorating economy gave greater resonance to the voices of those promoting dramatic political and social change and brought out into the streets many workers and squatters who would otherwise have stayed home. But it would be a vast simplification to say that economic decline caused this mobilization. It would be equally simplistic to see this mobilization as a short-term response to the thaw in military rule. The prior reshaping of definitions of what constitutes a political community of the poor, the extension of this definition from the factory to the shantytowns; the state's forcing nonincorporated shantytown organizations into opposition just as it incorporated what it hoped would be lasting corporatist bases; the entering into the shantytowns of a new set of religious and partisan actors; and the reshaping of parts of the popular political culture, away from clientelism and toward a rights-oriented militant version of citizenship—these were the causes of the social movement that took center stage in Peruvian politics during the final days of military rule.

Chapter Four

Lower-Class Politics
and Revived Civilian Rule

In March 1980 presidential and parliamentary elections were held for the first time in twelve years, bringing an end to Peru's longest period of military rule in this century. But the heritage of military rule under Velasco shaped lower-class politics after the state returned to civilian control. This heritage was nowhere clearer than in the persistence of a rights-oriented and confrontational politics among segments of the urban poor. The "new" movements engendered by the military state did not disappear when parties and interest associations returned to the open political arena. On the other hand, the return to civilian rule also opened up opportunities for clientelism.

Mobilization and Clientelism under Civilian Rule

Changes in urban popular-sector voting patterns after the return to civilian rule were among the most obvious indicators of a transformed lower-class politics. Between the 1930s and the 1960s voters in Lima's working-class districts supported candidates from reform-oriented, centrist, and conservative parties in proportions similar to those of voters in middle and upper-class districts (see chapter 2). But after the electoral hiatus of the military years, the residents of Lima's poor districts for the first time voted in patterns quite distinct from those of residents of higher-income districts.[1] Thus, in Lima, where one-third of Peru's population, and nearly two-thirds of its urban population, lived, class became a significant predictor of voting behavior for the first time.

In presidential elections candidates such as Alfonso Barrantes (United Left, 1985) and Alberto Fujimori (Change 90, 1990) received high levels of support from voters in Lima's lower-class residential districts but failed to attract substantial support from voters in wealthier districts. Table 3 compares some presidential elections from before and after the Velasco period. In both 1985 and 1990, support for the Left fell monotonically as district socioeconomic status rose, and support for the Right fell monotonically as district socioeconomic status fell. Although care is needed in interpreting these grouped data, the large differences in the magnitude of support for Left versus Right candidates in wealthy versus poor districts suggests a strong association between class and voting behavior.[2]

The new ideological profile of the urban poor was drawn especially sharply in municipal politics. Parties of the Left were the principal beneficiaries, particularly when the Left managed to maintain a unified coalition. This was true between 1981 and 1989, when most noninsurgent parties of the Left belonged to the United Left (IU) coalition. IU's national prospects dimmed greatly in 1989, when the coalition broke apart into two competing coalitions. While IU remained united, Alfonso Barrantes was elected mayor of Lima (1983–86), making him the first socialist mayor of a Latin American capital in which the national government was not also under socialist rule. Many district-level administrations in Lima were similarly controlled by the IU: ten of Lima's eleven poorest shantytown districts in 1983 elected mayors from the IU. The Left won the mayorship of all lower-class districts for at least part of the 1980s, but it won no municipal elections in middle- and upper-income districts. Independencia followed this pattern: the Left first assumed power of municipal government there in 1983 and retained it for a second term in 1986 and for a third term in 1989. (Survey results reported in chapter 6 will allow us to explore more deeply the meaning of lower-class voting behavior.)

Another indication of the sea change in lower-class politics was Sendero Luminoso.[3] Sendero began as a rural phenomenon in the

TABLE 3. Party Support in Presidential Elections
of 1963, 1985, and 1990, by Socioeconomic Status
of Residential Districts

Party	Socioeconomic status (%)		
	High	Middle	Low
1963			
AP	49.0	40.2	39.6
APRA	20.4	25.9	24.0
UNO	30.6	33.9	36.4
TOTAL	100.0	100.0	100.0
1985			
Left (IU)	14.2	23.9	30.9
Center (APRA)	44.3	53.0	55.3
Right (AP & PPC)	41.5	23.1	13.8
TOTAL	100.0	100.0	100.0
1990			
Center-Left (Fujimori)	30.1	51.0	62.2
Right (Vargas Llosa)	69.9	49.4	37.8
TOTAL	100.0	100.0	100.0

SOURCES: Henry A. Dietz, "Political Participation in the Barriadas: An Extension and Reexamination," *Comparative Political Studies* 18, no. 3 (1985): 323–55; Fernando Tuesta Soldevilla, *Perú político en cifras: Elite política y elecciones* (Lima: Fundación Friedrich Ebert, 1987); *El Nacional*, June 11, 1990.
NOTE: In the 1963 elections there were six high-, four middle-, and six low socioeconomic status districts. In the later elections there were nine high-, six middle-, and ten low-socioeconomic status districts (see Dietz, "Political Participation in the Barriadas.") The 1990 data are from the second-round runoff election.

1970s and remained basically rural for the first few years after 1980, when it declared itself in armed revolt. But as urban bombings, selective assassinations, "armed strikes," and torches outlining hammers and sickles burning on the hillsides surrounding Lima attest, by the late 1980s Sendero had become a potent urban force.

The rising power of Sendero in Peru's cities is traceable to two phenomena. One is the broader process of mobilization, the unintended consequence of the period of military rule that we have been following. This mobilization drew inspiration from various revolutionary rhetorics: the military government's rhetoric of a "Revolution in Participation," the Left's rhetoric of socialist revolution, and liberation theology's rhetoric of revolutionizing social relations to create the "kingdom of God on earth."

When the parties constituting the United Left turned to electoral politics in 1980, most of the coalition's growing social base accepted the view that the conquest of state power through the vote was the most effective path toward social change. But some felt defrauded. They found in Sendero a political organization that remained loyal to the promise of revolution.[4] Sendero's claim to be the only viable party committed to revolutionary change was bolstered when the United Left coalition split in 1989; Sendero's claim that Peruvian democracy was a sham was bolstered when Alberto Fujimori and the armed forces closed parliament and suspended the constitution in 1992.

Municipal Politics and Social Movements

In Peru in the 1980s, municipal government was a nexus between revived civilian political institutions and the new social movements of the urban lower classes. The experience of municipal government in Independencia illustrates the bifurcated patterns of mobilization and clientelism in Lima's lower-class residential communities under civilian rule; it also begins to explain why lower-class actors who took part in party and government life under civilian rule continued to turn to the politics of social movements.

The typical mayor and district council members in Lima's lower-class districts were local residents in their thirties whose activism and party ties went back to the mid-seventies. Some had begun their careers in parish youth organizations led by priests sympathetic to liberation theology; others had been recruited into political parties as high school or college students. Some became active in response to SINAMOS organizing. Independencia's two-term mayor Esther Moreno (1983–89) was a neighborhood activist of long standing and a cadre in a leftist party (the Partido Comunista Revolucionario, or PCR) whose party career soared with her election as mayor of a populous lower-class district. Moreno, who had become involved in community affairs through her parish youth group, was in her mid-thirties during her mayorship. She went on to be elected to the national senate in 1990.

Municipal government in Lima's shantytowns held the potential of unprecedented self-government for lower-class communities. But it also faced many difficulties, the most obvious being a scarcity of resources. With virtually no tax base, Independencia depended for most of its budget on transfers from the national government. The IU politicians in control of the municipal administration complained that the AP, APRA, and Cambio '90 (Fujimori) national governments held up the transfers, and fiscal deficits at the national level surely made the situation worse. In the mid-eighties, Independencia's annual budget was the equivalent of U.S. $140,000, or $0.87 per resident.

This scarcity of resources created great inefficiencies. The desk of a single government worker in a developed country contains more paper, pencils, staplers, and paper clips than did all the municipal offices of Independencia combined. Transportation to assemblies and community meetings in the higher reaches of the district depended on the one municipal Volkswagen bug, which was frequently in need of repairs or out of gasoline. Municipal leaders and staffs also lacked administrative experience, and highly ideological district councilors combined a strident rhetoric with an uninventive bureaucratic routine. The mayor herself, although pragmatic, was swamped by small matters.

A challenge facing Independencia's municipal leaders was to learn the skills of persuasion and consensus-building, skills that took on greater importance with the shift from a more purely movement politics to one of access to institutional power. Even admired leaders who, like Moreno, enjoyed close community ties were not always equal to this challenge. In early 1985, for example, a group of thirty families who found their housing inadequate took advantage of the March presidential elections to invade a hilltop that the district council had set aside for a park and athletic fields. The mayor visited the settlement and tried to convince the squatters of the need to preserve recreational spaces. The squatters were unconvinced, and the mayor was forced to flee, her car showered with stones. The incident illustrates that when Independencia's leaders failed to forge consensus, they could fall prey to the confrontational politics in which they had been schooled and which they continued to foster.

Indeed it would be a mistake to see these leaders as stepping out of the role of movement activists altogether. Among the *municipio*'s main functions was to rally protests against policies of the national government. The mayor and district councilors led marches with a variety of objectives, such as obtaining running water or electricity, reversing national economic policies, ending human rights abuses and political violence, to name just a few. This role was a more familiar one and reflected municipal leaders' perception of their government as the culmination of many years of popular mobilization. This perception was laid out in somewhat formalized terms in a municipal document:

Our administration is shaped by the conviction of representing a social movement originating in the Pampa de Cueva and Ermitaño land invasions, which gave birth to the district and which continued in many long days of struggle that our people have embarked on to obtain a more dignified life; [this social movement] turned later into the election of a municipal government that could authentically represent its interests. The United Left administration owes itself to this tradition of struggle, and the sum of actions and works completed have not a material meaning, but a profound social and political one.[5]

Some municipal leaders used marches and other protest actions against the national government as a way of deflecting attention away from their own failure to improve the conditions of poor people in Independencia. But others who worked energetically for local improvements also continued to lead marches at the national health ministry, sit-ins at the offices of the central water utility, and public demonstrations against national economic policy. They saw this as a realistic response to a political system that was still highly centralized, one in which local governments controlled few resources and had limited influence on areas of policy affecting their constituents.

The strategies and normative underpinnings of movements politics were deeply enough ingrained in Independencia that local government officials were under pressure to pursue them. When Independencia's United Left municipal leaders managed to improve local conditions while also expressing a vision of broader social transformation, they captured the allegiance of the community's rising generation of leftist activists. When they were ineffective in practical terms, or when they appeared to be managers uninspired by a vision of transformation, they lost this allegiance. But when they appeared to be corrupt, or when their involvement in political institutions appeared to be only self-serving, or when the various parties within the ever-fractious IU coalition became mired in conflict, the young turned actively against them.

Edgar Jimenez was a twenty-two-year-old medical student in 1985, active in a youth organization in Tawantinsuyu, a neighborhood of Independencia. Jimenez was the son of a construction worker. His ability to study medicine at a national university reflected the expanded education opportunities for lower-class students during the Velasco period; an older brother's salary as a bank teller supported his studies. Jimenez had read the works of José Carlos Mariátegui in his early college years and appeared to have a deep, almost personal relationship with that thinker: "When I read Mariátegui sometimes I feel that he's speaking directly to me." In 1985 Jimenez was an IU supporter; the mayor's office called on him to help organize events or to get some piece of information out to the neighborhood. But he also sympathized with the goals of Sendero Luminoso, although he was critical of its tactics. Unlike moderates in the IU national leadership, he refused to call *senderistas* "terrorists," referring to them rather as "guerrilleros."

In 1985, two years into Mayor Moreno's first term, Edgar Jimenez saw her as effective. When she ran for reelection a year later, he helped in her campaign but found her rhetoric increasingly "reformist." He was bitter, furthermore, about her former lieutenant mayor; Jimenez believed accusations that the lieutenant had siphoned public funds. By mid-1992 Jimenez found municipal government to be empty of democratic content, and IU's participation in the institution inspired by narrow partisan aspirations.

Three years earlier the IU had fractured, and no socialist candidate had been a serious contender in the 1990 presidential elections. In April 1992 Alberto Fujimori closed congress and suspended the constitution; municipal governments were allowed to continue functioning, but in July Fujimori announced that after their current terms ended (in November 1992), mayors would not be elected but instead would serve at his behest.[6] These developments coincided with Jimenez's drift away from IU and toward Sendero. By now a practicing physician in a public hospital—but still poor and living in Tawantinsuyu's El Cielo barrio—Jimenez agreed to help in a Sendero operation to light torches in the form of a hammer and sickle on a hillside overlooking Independencia.

Municipal Politics and Clientelism

Civilian rule opened up new opportunities and incentives for clientelism in Independencia. The municipal government itself sometimes sought clientlike relations with the outside and patronlike relations with its own population. An example of the former were Mayor Moreno's ties with Alfonso Barrantes, the mayor of all Lima in 1983–86. Barrantes was allied with a small group of relatively moderate parties within the IU coalition that included Mayor Moreno's. This meant that Moreno and Independencia received special attention from Barrantes and the Lima *municipio*. A road-paving program seemed to move forward faster in Independencia than in other poor residential areas of Lima in the mid-eighties. The Lima mayor's office donated to Independencia a statue of Michaela Bastidas, an eighteenth-century indigenous leader. Barrantes attended the unveiling of the statue on an island in the Tupac Amaru Highway, opposite Independencia's municipal offices.

Clientelism is defined as a two-way relation between unequal actors in which the trade occurring between the two benefits both but does not alter the power differential between them. The relationship between Moreno and Barrantes, and between the municipal governments of Independencia and Lima in the mid-1980s, was in some ways reminiscent of traditional patronage and clientelism, although now more partisan and less individualized. The patron, in this case Barrantes and his associates, selected beneficiaries through personal and partisan ties, and the "goods" they extended to their clients included some that were highly symbolic and meant to be interpreted as symbols of individual charity. This "gift-giving" was intended to elicit support, particularly electoral support.

The discussion above touched on clientelist features of the relationship between Independencia's residents and the municipal political leadership, mostly leftists. Ties between Independencia residents and conservative parties also displayed clientelist features. Two such parties existed in Peru in the early to mid-eighties: Popular Action (AP) and the Popular Christian Party (PPC).[7] The PPC had little ideological commitment to organizing lower-class communities; it tended to frame social issues in terms of the need to extend Christian charity to the poor. The PPC made some efforts, nonetheless, to attract lower-class voters. A few weeks before the 1985 presidential election a sign appeared over the doorway of a small home in the Ermitaño neighborhood of Independencia announcing a PPC "family dining hall," a version of the "popular dining hall" arising throughout Peru's urban areas. Neighbors whom I asked about the dining hall seemed skeptical about the intentions of its sponsors; immediately after the election the dining hall disappeared.

It may seem surprising that some residents and leaders I interviewed declared themselves to be PPC supporters or to be sympathetic with the party's goals and program. Carlos Velásquez, the secretary-general of El Cielo (whom we will meet again in chapter 5), was one of many supporters throughout the district who seemed to be drawn by a kind of identification with the lifestyle and values of the party's more typical supporters, members of the social and economic elite.

AP's relationship with Independencia and other shantytowns ran deeper than the PPC's. Since its inception AP has been a reformist party with populist and conservative leaders; the latter dominated the party after the period of military rule. Some of this reformist and populist tradition remained in AP despite a sharp rightward turn in the eighties. Both Belaúnde administrations (1963–68 and 1980–85) made efforts to cultivate a base among the urban and rural poor. The result in Independencia was a relatively small but still significant pool of supporters, people whom the party could recruit to be AP candidates in local elections.

Conservative party supporters tended to see their ties with political parties in instrumental terms. This is not to say that a certain worldview did not lie behind their support, but Independencia's conservatives tended to "float" among parties, establishing conditional and ephemeral relations with them. They expected clear and tangible benefits from political parties and were more capable than their more ideological neighbors of making and dissolving party affiliations over a short period.

The Church, Mobilization, and Clientelism

Striking parallels between the Catholic Church and leftist political parties were visible in Independencia after the return to civilian rule. Both had mobilized residents and stimulated a combative style of political action under the military regime. With the return to civilian rule they continued to play these roles. In the 1980s and 1990s nuns, clergy, and lay workers in Independencia continued to attempt to transform residents into assertive activists, conscious of their rights as citizens and deserving of special attention as poor people with urgent needs. Thus nuns and priests spoke of striving to "create consciousness" among the poor.

But the church, like leftist political parties, also displayed elements of a very different kind of relationship with the urban poor. Church workers faced a series of tensions and pressures that led them, against their will, to compromise their role as community mobilizers and shift to a role of patron or broker. One such pressure was competition from other religious groups, mainly Protestant evangelicals who proselytized actively. There was also competition from secular leaders and parties, which Catholic workers saw as competing for the time and energy of the most active residents. Nuns and priests also felt pressure from more conservative Catholic orders and from conservatives within the Catholic hierarchy.[8] As political violence intensified in the late 1980s, conservative bishops criticized nuns and priests for exacerbating social conflict. Politicians and the military echoed these accusations. Finally, as the economic crisis deepened, some of the church's most active followers began to withdraw from community affairs and spend more time trying to increase their income. Whenever numbers fell at community dining hall meetings, catechism classes, or open-air masses, church workers had to find new ways to bring their followers back.

This last pressure in particular led church workers in Independencia to compromise their self-stated mission of "creating consciousness" among the poor and focus instead on producing immediate benefits that would attract souls to their clubs and classes. Ana, a nun living in Ermitaño, recalled the following incident, which she clearly regretted. Early in the second Belaúnde government, leaders of a communal dining hall that Ana had helped to organize and continued to advise were invited to the presidential palace along with representatives of similar organizations from other parts of Lima. Ana accompanied the group. Violeta Correa, President Belaúnde's wife and the head of Popular Cooperation, the government's community-development agency, appeared at the event. When the Independencia group saw women from other districts surround Correa, bombarding her with requests for aid, they pressed Ana to do the same. The result was a donation of two industrial sewing machines and several rolls of fabric, which the dining hall members tried to use, unsuccessfully, to generate income.[9] The incident forced Ana to play a part she did not like, that of a church agent brokering goods, one-shot donations or gifts, from the president's wife.

The impact of church activists in Independencia was predictably ambiguous. While they continued to help form a subset of highly class-conscious activists, they also reinforced certain implicit currents of deference and "assistentialism" *(asistencialismo)*, a pejorative term used by church and political activists to mean a sort of charity-mongering that created ties of dependence.

To summarize, new social movements arose in Peru's cities when the Peruvian state, aspiring to install a participatory version of corporatism, set off a series of political, institutional, and cultural changes that affected poor people. But another by-product of this curious experience of military rule was the reproduction of a politics of clientelism. The return to civilian rule and electoral politics after 1980 allowed the more mobilized segments of the urban popular classes an enhanced access to institutionalized power. But clientelist ties between the state, parties, and the church, on the one side, and the popular sectors, on the other, were a resilient feature of Peruvian politics. Thus the political changes of military corporatist and then civilian rule left a strong but complex imprint on the urban popular sectors.

Part Two

Social Movements and Political Culture

Chapter Five

Clients and Radicals

Political Culture in Independencia

Las Flores Neighborhood Committee leaders had negotiated for years with SEDAPAL, the water utility, for running-water installations. But in 1985 dissidents formed a new water commission. The new commission complained that the neighborhood committee had agreed to too large a community contribution and had not bargained hard enough with SEDAPAL. The water commission's first act was to organize a rally outside SEDAPAL's offices. The neighborhood committee secretary-general did not take part: "How can we, the leaders, go shout at SEDAPAL? . . . We'd come off badly."

In the neighborhood of Condorcanqui, so high in the hills that it was engulfed by the clouds of Lima's infamous winter fog *(garua),* the Mixed Commission of Condorcanqui organized an open-air meeting in May 1986 to plan strategy for getting running water for the neighborhood. But a state of emergency, imposed by the APRA government after a Sendero attack, made the meeting illegal. At least that was the view of the Civil Guard captain who arrived with five other *guardias.* As the *guardias* milled about threateningly, billy clubs in hand, a speaker standing on the folding tables that served as a platform shouted into his bullhorn: "We pay taxes, it's our right to have water!"

Decades of clientelist ties between the state and the poor during the period of the oligarchic state, the new ethic of participation of the

Velasco era, and the reproduction of both clientelism and a movement politics with the revival of civilian government all encouraged
a complex political culture among the urban poor. This political
culture exhibited two distinct and conflicting patterns of belief and
action, which I have labeled *clientelism* and *radicalism.* I flesh out
clientelism and radicalism by looking at two aspects of how residents
view the political and social world around them: (1) their tendency to
identify horizontally or vertically in the class structure and (2) their
general ideologies, including views of the state, citizenship, and the
long-term goals of their political action. Next I explore the distinct
strategic and behavioral patterns implied in clientelism and radicalism, both of which derive from the attitudinal features presented
earlier. This involves looking at (3) actors' understandings of the role
of community leaders and (4) their perceptions of the propriety and
effectiveness of alternative strategies. Again, I stress not only that
Independencia's residents were distinguishable from one another in
relation to these four aspects of political culture but that these differences formed two identifiable patterns of worldview and strategic
orientation.

   It hardly bears repeating that this dichotomous political-cultural
scheme is a simplification of the worldviews and strategic inclina-
tions of a community of 160,000 people. Alternatively, we could be
guided by the Spanish saying *Cada cabeza es un mundo* (Every head
is a world) and describe the enormous variety of perceptions of
politics, class, the state, and strategies that one could surely uncover
in a community like this one. But my fieldwork convinced me that
the recent history of lower-class politics has created bifurcated patterns of political culture. What is more important, the bifurcated
quality of lower-class political culture is connected in specific and
traceable ways to the macropolitical history recounted in the first
part of this book.[1]

Field Method

This chapter draws on taped interviews with two dozen community
members and activists that I undertook after a year of participant-

observation in community organizations and Independencia's municipal government. I chose to interview residents who illustrated well the clientelist and radical currents that I found pervasive in the community; I also preferred to interview people whom I had observed in action in community affairs. Those I interviewed were also more active in leadership roles than were the more typical community members. The data in chapter 6, drawn from a random sample of Independencia's voters, are thus a useful complement to those contained in this chapter.

With one exception, interviews took place in the homes of the people interviewed.[2] All interviews were taped and later transcribed (see chapter 1). The interviews typically occurred during three visits and lasted, on average, about four hours. Except for housewives and others with flexible work schedules, I interviewed these local activists in their homes during weekends and weekday evenings. All of the names I use are pseudonyms.

The following ten residents appear frequently in the discussion:

Clientelists

Luis Cancho, president of Las Flores Neighborhood Committee and owner of a workshop producing small industrial machinery

Reynaldo Rojas, subsecretary of Las Flores Neighborhood Committee and Cancho's chief ally; ticket taker in a downtown movie theater

Virginia Verdera, secretary of "popular dining" hall and Ermitaño housewife and occasional washerwoman

Carlos Velásquez, secretary-general of El Cielo; a former bank teller, now a taxi driver

Clara Mayta, Villa El Angel, worker on a government-sponsored community development project in return for food; a former domestic servant, now washes clothes

Radicals

Lidia García, Las Flores Mothers' Club member and renegade member of the Las Flores Neighborhood Committee; housewife

Julia Romero, neighbor of García, former president of Las Flores Mothers' Club; once worked in a large fish-processing plant, now earns income washing clothes

Jorge Núñez, dissident in Las Flores Neighborhood Committee; worked in a large machine manufacturing plant but was forced into early retirement for union activism; now produces light industrial machinery under informal contracts

Leoncio Mamani, neighborhood committee leader in a community south of Las Flores; longtime candy factory employee

Rosario Huayta, women's club leader from El Ermitaño; formerly a seamstress in a small men's clothing factory

My description of alternative political cultural patterns focuses on the ways they were played out in Las Flores, the "young town" (population 800) within Independencia introduced in chapter 2, although other examples of similar patterns and tensions are drawn from other areas of Independencia. Indeed a deep rift lay close to the surface of Las Flores's community life, revealing itself with the slightest provocation; the rift was characteristic of many Independencia barrios, although it would come out in different ways. In Las Flores the principal actors in this conflict were, on one side, the officers of the local neighborhood committee and, on the other, a dissenting group of activists in the neighborhood committee and their allied mothers' club officers. About thirty women took part in the mothers' club, which received support from the Catholic Church. The mothers' club ran a "popular dining hall," in which the members collectively prepared meals, largely out of donated food, for their families.

Most immediately the conflict in Las Flores was over how, and on what terms, the community should obtain services such as water and electricity and land titles. The neighborhood committee officers and their followers favored developing friendly, personal ties with government agencies and shied away from confrontational negotiations; the mothers' club and neighborhood committee dissidents favored confronting the government and negotiating intensely. The conflict was also about the autonomy of the mothers' club from the neighborhood committee, an issue that focused on who should control the club's building. This conflict began in the period of military rule, when the neighborhood committee and the SINAMOS organizer tried to block construction of the building. In the 1980s tensions focused on who would control the building, with the members of the mothers' club holding that it belonged to them because they had built it (mainly with donations from church sources) and that therefore no one else should share in its use and administration. The neighborhood committee leadership believed that the "club's" building should serve the larger community, not the particular group of its members, that as the overarching community organization, the neighborhood committee should at least share in running the club's building. Conflict over all of these issues had divided the community for years, to the point where the neighborhood committee dissidents with their allied mothers' club eventually split off and formed their own neighborhood committee, which planned to seek legal recognition from the district.

This apparently local dispute was really a conflict over much larger issues (a fact that the antagonists were quick to recognize), namely, What is the place of workers in Peruvian politics? What kind of society should Peru be? and What does the state owe its citizenry? These questions lay behind the periodic conflicts that divided Las Flores and many other pueblos. They were questions that *pobladores* themselves asked and attempted to answer in discussions of national politics and struggles over local concerns.

Social Differences

In Las Flores, as in other communities, the social identification of activists varied: some were egalitarians, identifying themselves as workers or poor people who saw themselves as joined in unavoidable conflict with owners, managers, or "the rich." Others were more accepting of social hierarchy, acknowledging the power both of others over them and of themselves over their neighbors. These alternative views of social hierarchy and class relations were not tied strictly to the occupations of those who held them.[3] Both hierarchical clientelists and class-solidary radicals in Las Flores held a variety of occupations.

Activists such as García, Romero, and Núñez felt strong horizontal bonds with both workers and the poor. They saw themselves as poor people and interpreted the common neediness of the poor (for land, services, etc.) as a bond that united the residents of their community. As García put it, in contrast to rich neighborhoods, where services were readily obtained, "Here we don't have water, we don't have electricity, we don't have anything. Who's going to come knock on my door and say, 'Señora, here you are'? . . . that's what brings us together to fight *[eso es lo que nos une a nosotros a luchar].*"

Radicals' social egalitarianism and working-class consciousness surfaced frequently in discussions of their work lives and were shaped by exposure in their place of work to the "classist" labor unions that came to life in Peru under military rule. Leoncio Mamani, a neighborhood committee leader in a community near Las Flores, had in 1986 worked for twenty-seven years in a candy factory in the Avenida Colonial, part of Lima's industrial core. He belonged to a union in that factory that had been organized in the late 1970s by a cadre from a left-wing party. Mamani believed that a fundamental divide separated workers from company owners and managers:

> There is a limit: the worker is a worker, and the owner is an owner. [The worker] can't be in harmony with the owner. There are differences of classes . . . one is the bird of prey, and the other has to carry the other's load *[uno es el ave de rapiña, y el otro tiene que estar juntando para que el otro carga (sic)].*

Q: Why is harmony impossible?

A: Because the only thing that's important to the owner is exploitation. It doesn't matter to him whether the worker eats or sleeps . . . he uses the worker like a machine *[lo usa como una máquina].*

Mamani accused the current leaders of his union of having crossed the sharp dividing line between social classes; he used the analogy of divorce to explain the resulting psychological climate:

The current [union] leaders are perverse people, because they have cohabited permanently, the company with the union, and later they got divorced, like a husband and wife when they ask for a divorce. . . . The two, the company and the union, were walking around acting as if they loved the worker. [When I was a union leader I used to be careful to] respect the line, everyone has his line *[guardar la línea, todo el mundo tiene su línea].* If you're an owner, up to a point and no more, from that point forward you can't pass. I'm a worker, I won't pass beyond there. Don't do anything for me, not a single favor.

In fact Mamani's views permit a sort of archeology of perceptions of class relations among Peru's urban poor, both before the period of military rule and after. In the earlier period the company's management structure was smaller and less specialized, the owner himself running day-to-day operations. The union, under *aprista* influence, sought friendly ties with management. Mamani recalled with approval the benevolent paternalism of this earlier period:

You would say, "Señor Antonio, I need an advance, my wife is sick." [The owner would respond,] "Okay, how much do you need?" He would give conscientiously to the worker, he took good care of the worker *[lo atendían bien],* and the worker also worked with enthusiasm. Because that's what a worker needs, that they give him what he asks, and in exchange for that they can demand of him that he work with more will *[más voluntad].*

The views of class relations of Rosario Huayta, the Ermitaño Feminine Committee leader introduced in chapter 1, also reflected the views of earlier eras. Looking back on her experiences as a seamstress in a men's clothing factory in the 1950s, she also recalled the paternalistic framework of worker-owner relations in that earlier era, before exposure to activists from left-wing parties during the Velasco period converted her to a highly confrontational political strategy and acute sense of class conflict. In that earlier period she and her co-workers had been paid on a piecework basis; when the company received few contracts, its employees' incomes declined. But the tenor of worker-owner relations allowed the owner to find small ways of ameliorating these circumstances.

When we worked, they never denied us anything *[nunca nos negaban nada].* We would ask them when we didn't have any work to do, "Will you let us buy some scraps of cloth to make my husband a shirt?" [The owner] never prohibited this; he said, "Let's go down to storage and see if there is material to sell to you." When we went down we saw all the little scraps. The ladies said, "I want that for my children, how much is it?" "Take it," he would say. "Why shouldn't I give it to you? I know that if I deny you, you'll steal from me. Take it, just don't take too much."

Huayta, who later became an enthusiastic and combative community activist, had had quasi-familial ties with the factory's owners. The way she involved her employer in her marriage illustrates those ties:

The factory owner was the godfather of our marriage [*el padrino de nosotros de nuestro matrimonio*]. When we were to marry, I had a cousin who the Señora [the owner's wife] was close to, and the Señora asked my cousin if we had a patron yet. Our godfather was going to be an uncle of mine, but he said, "There's no problem" [i.e., in his being replaced by the owner]. So I got married, and they were the patrons; they were good people.

The seeking out of a patron and the intentional generalizing from the employer-worker relation to a broader web of friendship and quasi-familial ties are typical elements of the traditional working-class "culture of personal dependence" that Stein identified with early-twentieth-century Lima. But in 1986 Huayta was recounting a piece of personal history that she would be unlikely to repeat. Her friendly acceptance of patronage here stood in tension with her own combativeness and anti-elite views and strategies. Growing class consciousness coming out of contact with unions and parties did not lead Huayta and Mamani to reject completely their past clientelism; rather, they saw it as natural in an earlier era in which workers had had to demand less to receive fair treatment from employers. Others whom I interviewed experienced a conversion that was more fundamental, and they condemned what they saw as their own earlier passivity and overdeference (see below).

A personal or family involvement with labor unions was an important part of the pattern of experiences that led shantytown residents to a combative, rights-conscious political outlook. Many unionized workers saw themselves as indebted to fellow workers for their training and support, and their loyalty to the union symbolized their recognition of this debt. Jorge Núñez, a dissident member of the Las Flores Neighborhood Committee, was an ambitious young worker who sought support from the management of the factory in which he worked. After Núñez finished a course in industrial design, the factory owner offered him a raise but told him to leave the union. But Núñez refused: fellow workers had taught him their skills during his apprenticeship, and he was willing to sacrifice higher wages to preserve that bond. "Now, if I left the union, how would my coworkers treat me? They taught me [*Yo me he formado de ellos*]. I learned watching them cut metal strips; when they worked their tools I went along and watched and asked questions, and they explained to me. And now that I've learned and I went out to get training, am I going to leave them? No, I can't."

Class consciousness of this sort was absent from the words of officials in the Las Flores Neighborhood Committee, as well as from those of leaders with a clientelist mentality in other parts of Independencia. Most either were exposed to APRA-affiliated unions prevalent before the rise of New Left and Communist Party–affiliated unions in the 1970s (this was the case of Carlos Velásquez) or were nonunionized workers (Reynaldo Rojas, Virginia Verdera, Clara Mayta). The owner of the movie theater where Reynaldo Rojas, subsecretary of the Las Flores Neighborhood Committee, worked owned several theaters; in all but Rojas's the employees were unionized. Rojas preferred his theater's system of "direct dealing" (*trato directo*) between workers and the owner to avoid "problems or anything public."

In activities related to their neighborhood committee, men like Rojas and Cancho identified more closely with the "gentlemen," "engineers," or "professionals" with whom they were in contact at government ministries and public utilities than with their poor neighbors. These leaders described Las Flores as poor, but they spoke of their community as if from a distance. Rojas spoke of the "needs of the people" thus: "There are so many people who don't have stable work, there are mothers who are single women, there are widows, there are even old people, so the community leader has to look out for all of them." The categories of people in need that Rojas spoke of—the unemployed, women, and older residents—were not categories he fell into. Clientelist leaders like Rojas saw themselves as representing the poor community without identifying with its poverty.

In contrast to the gentle paternalism of Reynaldo Rojas, other leaders were hostile to their poor neighbors, despite the similarity of the latter's economic circumstances to their own. Despite having lost his bank job twenty years earlier and barely keeping his family fed by driving a taxi, Carlos Velásquez still identified with a middle class to which he could once aspire:

In a bank, beginning with clothing, you have to be well dressed, you have to live more or less in a presentable place. . . . It's not like being a worker, who can live on top of a hill, can go to work with worn-out shoes. . . . Because of your social position *[Por el mismo roce social],* you have to deal with other kinds of people, you have to educate yourself more, choose your friends. It's not like being a worker. . . . In your social life also, a worker can go to a *cantina* and get drunk, but a [white collar] employee can't do that. You always have to be careful about your prestige *[cuidar su prestigio].*

This sense of being in but not of the poor community created discord between clientelists in leadership positions—both Cancho and Velásquez were neighborhood committee presidents—and other residents. In prior periods, before clientelism had to compete with radicalism, perhaps it was easier for these leaders to sustain harmonious relations with their communities. By the time of my study these leaders felt isolated from their constituents, whom they in turn regarded with disdain. In Las Flores they saw themselves as exercising a sort of *noblesse oblige* by assuming community leadership, and they were bewildered and angered when constituents criticized their actions. Clientelist leaders repeatedly complained of the personal financial sacrifice that being a leader entailed, of having to pay for documents and bus fares. Their critics inferred from this that the leaders were better able than their more impoverished neighbors to assume this sacrifice and that they hoped to gain status by flaunting their expenses.

In Las Flores, perceptions of social hierarchy led to periodic conflict. In the midst of a confrontation with the Mothers' Club, Luis Cancho's wife shouted, "Ignorant, dirty people! Go wash your faces!" Carlos Velásquez, the leader from the nearby community, spoke in a similarly disparaging way of his fellow *pobladores*. One evening our interview was interrupted by a neighbor, a woman who had come to place her name on a community register. The woman was deferential toward Velásquez: she addressed him simply as "Señor" and looked at the ground as she spoke. After she left Velásquez complained of having to coax his constituents to act: "It's ignorance. . . . They live like animals, it's true. So a leader has to fight, has to coax them like a child, like a baby, 'Listen, come on, I'll register you.'"

The State, Citizenship, and the Goals of Political Action

Few whom I interviewed spoke habitually in abstract ideological terms, but Independencia's radicals were more prone to abstract formulations than were clientelists. Central to the radicals' political views was a strong sense of citizens' rights, especially of the rights of poor people before the state; indeed, it was the government, more commonly than the dominant economic classes, to whom confrontation-oriented leaders saw themselves as principally opposed. Independencia's radicals believed that they lived under a class state. In the words of one resident, the state "inclines itself" more toward "people who have money and who already have all the comforts, and tries to give them more comforts, because [the state] knows that it can get more money out of [the rich]." But radicals rejected this class state: they thought it was both unjust and changeable. Or at least they thought that even if the state's core predisposition toward helping "the rich" could not be changed, its external behaviors could. Independencia's radicals thought that their version of pressure politics could induce the state to behave in a more democratic fashion, that is, with a greater responsiveness, albeit a forced responsiveness, to poor people like themselves.

Independencia's radicals frequently asserted that poor communities transferred value to the state through taxes and therefore had a right to demand things of value in return. In fact they were remiss if they failed to demand valued goods in exchange for their taxes. This exchange view of citizenship was invoked against the idea, which originated in the period of the oligarchic state, that government support for the poor was a form of philanthropy. Julia Romero, a Las Flores activist, summed up this view when she insisted that running water was not a gift: "We don't want them to give water to us as a gift . . . it's not an alm, we pay all our taxes."

The revival of district municipal government in the 1980s allowed confrontational leaders to make this financial link between the state and lower-class taxpaying citizens more obvious. Leoncio Loja, Independencia's AP mayor (1980–83), was commonly accused of corruption. One radical complained: "We felt [the corruption] because it was our community's money, from us ourselves, because all taxes that we pay, we are conscious, have to be for the benefit of us ourselves." This understanding of the difference between private and public monies was echoed by Josefina Ruiz, an illiterate, middle-aged highland migrant and a militant in a Marxist political party: "[Under the current United Left administration] the municipality understands that [its budget] belongs to the people. It doesn't come out of the municipality's pocket, from the mayor's pocket; it's the property of the population, we all give our support. Now that money is invested in us, which is something that no other mayor has done." Unremarkable as these condemnations of official venality may seem, there is a striking contrast between this vision of the relationship between private and public resources, and between the state and citizens, and the earlier (and still existing) images.

The notion that a state, although basically hostile to the poor, can be forced into greater evenhandedness through community activism is linked to the idea of participation, a key concept for radicals. It was so encompassing an idea that we can speak of an ideology of participation in Lima's shantytowns. The prevalence of the word *participation* in local political discourse again links the radical political subculture to the Velasco period, when the term gained currency: the Velasco regime defined its method as a "Revolution of Full Participation" *(Revolución de Participación Plena).*

Participation was a concept relevant to religious as well as political life. Just as one ought to be an active participant in the community's political life, one ought also to strive for full participation in religious life. Julia Romero saw her religious life as acquiring meaning only after it became participatory, in her case after she met Father Stephen, a priest who wore lay clothing. Only then, in her own view, did she begin to shed her passive attitude toward church authority and ceremony.

[In the highlands] I used to go to mass, and I liked to show respect for the priests. . . . For us in my pueblo the priest is the highest authority. We used to respect them a lot. But before there was no participation *[antes no había participación]*. When I lived in Rímac [a working-class district near the center of Lima] I used to go to mass every Sunday. There I was thinking all was well, but at bottom it wasn't true.

Real participation meant actively projecting oneself into civil and religious affairs. And the shift from passivity to meaningful participation was linked in Romero's experience to questioning authority, in this case religious authority.

Radical activists believed that participation should change the attitudes of people toward their social and political surroundings in addition to allowing the poor to acquire the material services their communities needed. Participation should "create consciousness" *(crear conciencia)*, or force participants to "become conscious" *(tomar conciencia)*, and allow people to "see reality" *(ver la realidad)*. Creating consciousness and seeing reality meant acquiring a more critical attitude toward the state, social hierarchy, and established authorities. These changes in consciousness also implied shedding an individualistic understanding of one's problems, coming to see one's personal difficulties as connected to broader social problems. A Las Flores Mothers' Club activist explained: "I began participating in [the club's] meetings and since then started realizing that my problems are not mine alone: they exist at the district level or, you could say even—who knows?—at the world level. It's just that everyone is in his own place *[solo que cada uno está en su sitio]*."

Occasionally radicals in Independencia framed their current struggles in terms of general relations of power and exploitation. Members of the Las Flores Mothers' Club understood the conflict between themselves and the neighborhood committee as one of the powerful trying to perpetuate their power; they drew parallels between the committee's power and the social power of exploitative classes. Their rhetorical salvos drew on Peruvian history, echoing the "critical idea" of that history, as Portocarrero and Oliart put it, that entered the public school curriculum with the Velasco education reform. Lidia García of the Las Flores Mothers' Club, who was a high school student in the 1970s, draws on a reading of Peru's colonial past to explain the Las Flores secretary-general's motives as follows:

[The secretary-general's] character is one of imposing, . . . [it's like] the time of the Spanish, no? When the most powerful took his three or four vassals and ordered them around *[el más poderoso agarraba sus tres o cuatro lacayos y los mandaba]*. Or a whole population came and governed however they liked . . . I think that [the secretary-general] wants to do that here. He feels within his rights and thinks that we are going to consent. But he doesn't realize that things have changed, things are different.

What broader goals did confrontational leaders see themselves as working toward, and what broader meaning did they give their activism? Rosario Huayta saw the significance of her activism in personal terms; she stressed her own transformation into an effective political actor through learning leadership skills and a new commitment to community affairs. When she was asked about the long-term goals of her work, Huayta responded:

The objective that I have achieved in my life is to have constructed the Health Center. That was a triumph, the first time in my life that I was able to successfully negotiate *[gestionar]* something that wasn't for me but for the service of the whole community . . . for me that was something big. I've told the ladies [club members] that from them I learned to demand *[reclamar]* what is just, and to confront many problems.

Others stressed the connection between their efforts and larger goals, such as making Peru an egalitarian society. In a rare moment, Julia Romero spoke of the kind of society she and others in the mothers' club wanted to create. Unaccustomed to the language of abstraction, she groped noticeably for her words:

What we señoras want—the reason we organize ourselves—is to be able, we hope with time, our objective is that there should be a new society, a change. . . . We hope that there will be a change [so that it will be] like this: we all eat or no one eats *[todos comemos o todos no comemos]*. But right now there are others who eat and others of us who don't eat. That's bad, from my way of looking at things it shouldn't be that way.

Josefina Ruiz, a longtime Marxist party member, gave a more ideological turn to her explanation of her ultimate goals. The personal element disappeared; characteristically, "I" became "we." Even though she was illiterate, her speech was ideologically more fluid than Romero's; but her ideas were similar:

Our analysis is, the only way we can reform this country is seeing that there aren't bosses, there aren't any people, exploiters *[que no hayga (sic) patrones, que no hayga personas, explotadores]*. Making this Peru a socialist Peru, where there won't be bosses or exploiters. That's what we're aiming for, that Peru be reformed, but it has to be a socialist Peru *[pero que sí un Perú socialista]*. And we want people to become conscious *[Y que nosotros la conciencia queremos que el pueblo tome]* so that we can all make this change, because now we're so exploited.

The way radicals described the broader goals of political action is significant for two reasons. First, the very words they used reflected some of the sources of the political worldview that established these goals, among them Marxist political parties and church organizations with strong egalitarian messages. Second, these three different expressions of goals are all ambitiously transformative, describing a transformation of the self (Rosario Huayta) or imagining a transformation of society (Josefina Ruiz, Julia Romero). If clientelism called for small material improvements through confined exchanges, the radical vision was much more utopian, even spiritual.

Clientelists were less given than were radicals to using abstract language to describe their goals and actions, language that involved thinking toward an indefinite future and an imagined social transformation. As conservatives, they found it less necessary than radicals did to mentally feel out an alternative social order, a process that by definition requires abstraction from the present. Their ultimate goals centered on the physical improvement of their communities, defined literally as the area of their neighborhoods.

Sometimes the goal was to obtain permanent infrastructural improvements (the more common goal), sometimes one-shot handouts from the government or other patrons. Virginia Verdera, the secretary of a "popular dining hall" in Ermitaño, illustrates this latter goal. At a membership meeting Verdera came into conflict with the nun running a network of dining halls when the nun asked the members to accept a smaller ration of bread for each dining hall so that more could enter the network. The nun stated her view in a characteristic "radical" way, connecting local actions to the resolution of broad social problems: "We know that we are poor not because our society is poor but because of an unequal distribution of resources. We should demonstrate equality here, just as we fight for it in society."

Verdera looked on unhappily, then spoke. "We're always getting less and less," she said. "It's almost Christmas, and we'll eat less. I remember the old days when at Christmas the priests would come and give us *panetones* (fruitcakes)." Verdera was referring to the traditional gift, especially of factory owners to workers and of politicians to shantytown residents, which constituted almost a cliché of paternalistic philanthropy in Peru.

But despite this very tangible and practical emphasis of clientelist leaders and their followers, one could glean from some of their statements implicit views of what society should look like. For example, one criticism they frequently leveled against their more confrontational neighbors was that the latter were *resentidos,* people full of resentment. This pejorative term was used to describe people who complained about poverty and inequality; the implication was that it was wrong to complain about these things and that a certain acceptance of one's lot was the appropriate attitude for humble people to hold.

When clientelist leaders and activists did offer general and normative reflections, they often focused on community self-reliance. This focus resonated with that of conservatives like Pedro Beltrán, who in the 1950s extolled self-help for poor communities and homeowners (see chapter 2). The ability of poor communities to pull themselves up by their bootstraps, without assistance from the state or others, was an idea that ran through clientelist leaders' view of their community's history; sometimes they described it as simply a necessary consequence of governmental neglect, but more often they saw it as praiseworthy. Las Flores's Reynaldo Rojas spoke proudly of community projects achieved "with the sacrifice of the population, without the help of any government or anything else, only with the effort of the whole population."

This ideology of community self-help found some resonance in the larger population because, in fact, its investment in housing and services, both in material and in labor, had been enormous. But the ideal of self-help ran contrary to the basic thrust of patron-client relations between shantytown leaders and the state. Clientelist leaders extolled community initiative, but at the same time they sought out assistance from individuals within the bureaucracy. And the measure of their merit was their success in attracting patronage, not in organizing up-from-the-bootstraps local efforts. Their emphasis on community self-help can in part be explained as a rhetorical stratagem aimed at those very bureaucrats who, in the tradition of Pedro Beltrán, preferred to think of community development in poor areas as resulting from indigenous initiative. But it also formed a very basic part of the clientelists' worldview.

How Should a Leader Act?

Distinct patterns of community leadership flowed from clients' and radicals' differing social self-identifications as well as from their distinct views of the state, citizenship, and the goals of political action. Some leaders aggressively identified themselves as poor people and workers; others identified themselves with social and political elites. For radical leaders, showing solidarity with other workers was integral to leadership; they saw themselves as workers and poor people leading others like themselves. An example comes from members of the Las Flores Mothers' Club, who became caught up in the wave of union activism in the late 1970s even though they were not union members. When I interviewed them a decade later, they proudly recalled locking strikebreakers inside a secondary school during a teachers' strike. In Julia Romero's view, this kind of activism was valuable not only because it produced results but also as a sign of solidarity and combativeness: "Whenever people have made demands . . . we have participated, we've supported them, we've even gone on marches with no reason [i.e., when the results didn't affect us] so that people would realize that this is a place where people fight."

Confrontational leaders constructed their authority around the claim that they were poor people exactly like the poor people they represented: they had nothing material to offer to their constituents. Any material benefits to the community would have to come from hard-nosed bargaining by leaders, backed up by active pressure from their constituents.

Radical leaders and their supporters placed great value on negotiating hard with the state to get a good deal for services and other resources. Romero recalled telling the members of the Las Flores Mothers' Club, after they elected her president, "I couldn't offer them anything, nothing, because I am a woman just like [them], I don't have money. . . . If we want to do something, we'll do it together." One of the radicals' main criticisms of clientelists was that they had too concessionary an attitude in negotiations and failed to *regatear* (haggle, bargain). The club's treasurer complained that Luis Cancho, the committee's secretary-general, was "servile" and "doesn't like to struggle": "He likes to say 'it costs me so much for this thing and I allow myself the luxury of paying for it.' But he doesn't like to bargain." Hard bargaining to arrive at a just price was thus the radical leaders' approach to representing poor communities.

The clientelists' authority, in contrast, was constructed around their social status and reputation for wealth. They emphasized their ability to absorb the incidental costs of transportation to government ministries, fees for documents, and missed work. Whereas radical leaders insisted that they had nothing material to offer, clientelists found ways to make clear the financial sacrifices they endured.

The conflict between Las Flores's competing water commissions flowed from these differences between radical and clientelist economic approaches to community leadership. The original water commission, made up of leaders of the neighborhood committee, and SEDAPAL, the municipal water authority, had agreed in 1985 to a financing scheme in which the community bore significant costs for installing running water. Their critics wanted the leaders to negotiate a reduced community contribution and announced that they would form their own water commission to deal with SEDAPAL independently. Lidia García's opinion illustrates the loss of consensus over status spending:

If the secretary-general feels capable of acting like a millionaire, what is he doing here? *[Si el secretario general se siente en capacidad de dársela de millonario, qué hace acá?]* Why doesn't he go live in San Isidro or Miraflores [elite residential districts of Lima]. . . . In every meeting we have, that's the first thing he says to us, that he's the leader with his pockets full of money. What he means is that he doesn't owe the people anything, that if he's the leader it's because to be a leader you need money for transportation.

On the other side, the original water commission could not simply turn to a more confrontational strategy and hope to retain the friendly relationship they had cultivated with SEDAPAL officials. In the words of Luis Cancho, "The [SEDAPAL] engineers say, 'Those people cry a lot, they bother us a lot, you have to attend to them.' . . . [The members of the new water commission] say, 'Let's go fight SEDAPAL, let's go shout.' How can we, the leaders, go shout at SEDAPAL? What would they say to us? We'd come off badly *[quedaríamos mal]*." Cancho's dismay reflected a real dilemma. Because his leadership style was based on cultivating friendly ties with government personnel, and because his authority in the community was based on his special ability (through wealth, social standing, and knowledge) to get things done, asking him to "go fight . . . and shout at SEDAPAL" was the equivalent of asking him to give up his claims to leadership. Furthermore, because he viewed himself as fundamentally similar to the professionals at the water utility, and fundamentally different from the lower-class residents of his neighborhood, taking part in the second water commission's strategies would have violated his own sense of who he was and where he fit into his society. Thus, for normative, psychological, and strategic reasons, the practices of "struggle" were simply unavailable to Luis Cancho and others like him.

The different values that radicals and clientelists attached to broad community participation also had strategic implications. Radicals saw participation as a good in itself, and as a route to meaningful community life; effective leaders, therefore, stimulated a maximum of activism among their constituents. Movement leaders who were subsequently elected to office proved their value by continuing to promote movement-style participation. Rosario Huayta said about Independencia's mayor, "I've talked with a lot of neighbors, and just about a majority agrees that IU should continue, the mayor should continue [in power], mainly [because] she participates and makes all of us participate with all of the problems that there are."

Clientelists opposed broad community activism: it cut across the grain of their own authority, which rested on the perception of their special wealth, connections, or other resources. They identified mentally with the officials who would be the object of pressure strategies, and therefore they probably felt the same discomfort that these officials felt (and were meant to feel) when they faced angry groups of protesters. Hence their preference for strategies that centralized all contact with government officials in their own hands. As Reynaldo Rojas put it, "The leader himself has the job of doing all the paperwork, until the ultimate consequences"; if he runs into some difficulty, "that's what membership meetings are for." Instead of encouraging noisy participation, leaders should direct *(conducir)* their constituents: "We have to direct them in everything having to do with paperwork, and leave everything all finished for them."

Against radicals' call for broad community participation, then, clientelists saw leaders as socially select and insisted that only a few members of any community had the knowledge (especially of the bureaucracy) and the financial resources necessary to lead. The followers of these clientelist leaders shared this view. Clara Mayta, for example, was a resident of Villa El Angel, the southernmost neighborhood in Independencia. Mayta's activism had peaked during the land invasion that formed the community in the early 1960s; she described herself as engaged since then only in work (as a domestic servant and, later, with her husband, as a live-in guard at several construction sites) and bringing up her children. When I asked her how her community chose its leaders, she replied that "we look for a person who would know *[una persona que sepa]*, so that he can go find out what's going on." Mayta herself appeared ill-informed about national politics and her community's past; she was unsure, for example, about who the leaders of the military regime had been or whether SINAMOS had been active in her neighborhood.[4]

Mayta's perception of leaders as a natural elite reflected real inequalities in knowledge, experience, and attentiveness to community affairs between leaders and people like her. She saw the greater knowledge of others as reflecting not experience or attentiveness but their greater innate abilities. This perception contrasts sharply with the interpretation of radicals like Rosario Huayta of political knowledge and skills as learned, coming out of the experience of action itself. Hence Huayta's recollection of herself as someone who "was shy and thought that what I was going to say would seem stupid to other people" until she met up with the organizer who "gave me a good education."

Political Strategies

Radicals' approach to political strategy, like their approach to leadership, followed naturally from their stress on equality, class solidarity, and participation and from their perception of the state as a class state that nevertheless could (and ought to) be pressured into a more evenhanded treatment of the poor. The logic of radicals' confrontational strategy was to extract services and concessions by exerting pressure on powerful actors, principally the state. Whereas clientelists cultivated relations with government officials that combined friendship and a sense of shared enterprise, radicals tried to provoke fear. Radicals saw little value in softening their tactics with an eye toward future concessions from actors they regarded as opponents. They preferred to build their relationship with opponents on the latter's fear of naked pressure rather than on trust and amiability. Although most leaders who used pressure tactics at some point joined in low-key discussions, their basic instinct was toward antagonism. This instinct could not have been more at odds with that of clientelists, who avoided high-pressure, antagonistic strategies in all situations: such tactics violated key pieces of their worldview and social identity and were therefore absent from their strategic repertoire.

Luchar (to struggle) and *pelear* (to fight), as well as *reivindicar* (to claim that which one rightly deserves) and *concientizar* (to raise consciousness), were key verbs in the radicals' political vocabulary; *marcha* (march), *demanda,* and *reclamo* (demand) were key nouns. Confrontational leaders and activists adopted the language of the *lucha* with great intensity. Taken out of context, one district council member's account of the activists' campaign for water, health clinics, and better transportation could make it sound as if there were a perpetual insurrection: "Many times we have taken the transportation ministry, the health ministry, we have taken the housing ministry, SEDAPAL [the water utility]—that was commonplace." But even if they did not "take" the ministries in a military sense, the feeling the marchers hoped to instill in ministry personnel was one of frontal attack.

The strategy of *lucha,* or struggle, was consistent with many residents' sense of the Peruvian state as representing the rich, the *gente acomodada* (comfortable people), whom they viewed as hostile to the needs and interests of the poor. As we have seen, however, radicals regarded the state as permeable to lower-class demands if they were pressed with sufficient intensity. Therefore, radicals were set on

violating the etiquette of state-*poblador* relations. Fernando González, a dissident Las Flores Neighborhood Committee member, explained that "when you go and make demands *[reclamos]* before the
central government, it makes them uncomfortable *[les incomoda a
ellos]*. Under no circumstances do they want poor people to go in a
group to make demands. They get scared, it makes them uncomfortable; they prefer that only one or two leaders go to do the paperwork."
Behind the radicals' strategy lay the belief that poor people could only
succeed by breaking traditional rules of etiquette and intimidating
state actors.

Whereas radicals spoke of fighting, clientelists spoke of making
requests; in situations where radicals organized noisy marches, clientelists preferred small, restrained meetings with government personnel, whose friendship they skillfully cultivated. One officer of the
Las Flores Neighborhood Committee spoke with pride of his knowledge of the bureaucracy and his ties to government personnel. When
the new Las Flores leadership came to office in 1981 and began by
petitioning *(gestionando)* for property titles,

[We went] to various offices and spoke with various engineers, etc., places
where we knew already that we should go and talk with an engineer. . . . We
took maps [and said], We're leaders, we live in such and such a place *[vivimos
en tal sitio]* . . . we told the history of the community also. Well, [the engi-
neer] said to us, on such and such a day I'm going to go, because I have to
see where you people live. And that day the engineer came; he was a
marvelous old man *[un viejito maravilloso]*.

Developing friendly personal relations with engineers like this
"marvelous old man" was useful for obtaining land titles and running
water; it also affirmed the clientelist leader's sense of his or her own
superior social standing with regard to the broader community of the
poor. When the two leaders returned for a second visit,

We went in just like that *[tranquilo llegamos]*, we sat down, [the engineer]
introduced us to his secretary, saying, "These gentlemen are leaders from
the pueblo Las Flores, so please whenever they come and ask for me or
bring documents, attend to them for me immediately," because we had told
him about the community's suffering and everything *[ya nosotros habíamos
contado el sufrimiento del pueblo y todo]*. "So don't make these gentlemen
sit around: let me know immediately that they're here, even if I'm busy let

me know they're here, and their papers shouldn't sit on your desk *[no deben estar allí permaneciendo]* but rather immediately you should do their paperwork."

Acting on these conceptions of leadership, whether the radical or the clientelist version, created anxieties. Radical leaders enjoyed their activism; it was reflected in the feelings of people like Huayta that they were engaged in "something big." But they faced repression and political violence, increasingly as the 1980s progressed. The anxiety of the clientelists, on the other hand, was connected to the challenge that radicalism had brought to their prestige and to the solitude imposed by their leadership style. They complained of isolation from their neighbors, but at the same time they pointed to this isolation as evidence of their special political role. Carlos Velásquez's words, which alternate between pride in his isolated position and loneliness, illustrate the anxieties of the clientelist: "No one ever goes with me anywhere. I do everything by myself. I have to say that with complete pride, I walk alone, other leaders don't want to work. No one wants to work. Everywhere I'm known all by myself *[En todas partes soy conocido solito]*."

In chapter 6 I analyze the sources of both strands of the bifurcated political subculture—radicalism and clientelism. The lives of several residents suggest that certain experiences and institutions played a role in disseminating the newer pattern. Leoncio Mamani shows that labor unions, like the "classist" union in his candy factory, can undermine the legitimacy of harmony in worker-owner relations, molding militant workers, who then bring their militancy to shantytown affairs. Julia Romero illustrates the transforming impact of those in the church who were anti-authority, such as the young priest who disdained his robes and drummed up an activist form of religious participation. Romero also illustrates how the military's rhetoric of participation could be turned back against the regime. Rosario Huayta went from being a seamstress who gratefully gathered up the scraps of cloth, always with her employer's consent, to leading groups of shouting women into the ministry of health. She attributed her changed consciousness to her contact with another new kind of activist of the military period, the middle-class university student and party cadre. Finally, we heard echoes of the "critical idea" of Peruvian history and society, also introduced under military rule, in local understandings of power and exploitation.

But clientelism persisted. It consisted in a personalistic understanding of the relationship between poor communities and the state, an image of community improvement as a matter of communities pulling themselves up by the bootstraps, state assistance as charity, and community leadership as the purview of the socially select. These beliefs are consistent with the understanding of the ties between the poor and the state promulgated under the oligarchic state, and sometimes still by the Peruvian state, parties, and the church.

Chapter 6

Political Culture
and the Mass Public

This chapter addresses two sets of questions. The first set concerns the relevance to the mass population of patterns among leaders. Does survey analysis confirm the existence of a rift in popular political culture in Peru between "radicals" and "clients"? Can this rift be seen in Independencia's mass adult population? Or are better explanations available? If we were to find, for instance, that the mass public's attitudes toward the state, social classes, and political strategies did not follow the patterns suggested in the client-radical dichotomy, this finding would at the least raise doubts about this dichotomy's relevance to the political culture of the mass public (as opposed to activists and leaders). Perhaps poor people have no particular preference, for instance, for confrontational actions over clientelism, but use these strategies selectively according to the situation at hand. If this were the case, we would not expect to find an association between strategic preferences and views, say, of the value of class solidarity or the state.

The second set of questions concerns the link between contemporary and historical patterns. Do data about individuals confirm the historical sequence, laid out in chapters 2 through 4, of changes leading to the rise of a new social movement among the urban poor? Were the historical shifts underscored in the first part of this study—a state-induced realignment of the labor movement and political parties, the appearance of new sets of outside actors in the shantytowns, the diffusion of the "critical idea" through the public schools—indeed responsible for growing social movements?

85

Thus, even if we find evidence of a client-radical split in the attitudes of Independencia's mass voting public, several alternative explanations of this split are plausible. I have argued that radicalism in Peru's urban social movements was the product of recent historical changes, unfolding since the early 1970s. But this view could be wrong: perhaps every age has its radicals and its clients. Radicals and clients could be, not people belonging to different subcultures, but people at different stages of the life cycle. Or there may be enduring differences among shantytown residents that have nothing to do with the Velasco experience. Perhaps the split is based on gender: men and women may be socialized differently in early life. Or perhaps differences in income in communities that are poor but not homogeneously so account for different political outlooks.

The data presented in this chapter will help us answer these questions. They are the result of a sample survey of the voting population of Independencia that I conducted in May and June 1986. Lists of Independencia's voters, provided to me through the National Electoral Registry, provided the sampling frame. There are reasons for believing that these lists are fairly complete. Voting is compulsory in Peru after the age of eighteen, and citizens are required to carry evidence of current registration. The *libreta electoral,* or voting card, is the universal identification document that adults are required to produce in a variety of situations, akin to the North American driver's license, and lower-class Peruvians are at some risk if this document is missing or out of date. The National Electoral Registry's lists were comprehensively updated in July 1984. Those who came of age after that time were required to register on a continuing basis and therefore would have been included in the lists from which the sample was drawn.

The voting lists were compiled in loose-leaf "books" of registration forms, each containing 200 sheets, one per voter. In 1986 there were 371 books of voters registered to vote in Independencia; thus, the district contained about 74,200 voters. The National Electoral Registry personnel agreed to select three voters per book, using skip numbers that I supplied. Deaths and moves out of Independencia reduced the original group of 1,113 to an effective sample of 985 voters. In order to ensure a high response rate, I hired and trained a group of high school and college students from Independencia, who knew its neighborhoods and would appear familiar enough to inspire confidence in respondents (although no student was assigned an interview with anyone whom she or he knew personally). The students successfully interviewed 882 (90 percent) of those selected; the remaining 103 (10 percent) refused to answer questions. The survey instrument, which is translated and reproduced in the appendix, was pretested in two neighborhoods in the extreme southern portion of Independencia; to avoid contamination, I excluded these neighborhoods from the final sample.

The Political Culture of Voters: Clientelism versus Radicalism?

The survey discovered the importance respondents gave to ties among workers, their preferences for strategies in community action, and their views of the state or national government. Voters were asked whether they would accept a job in a factory on condition that they not join the union of factory workers. The question was intended to distinguish between people who felt strongly enough about worker solidarity that they would make (at least hypothetically) some sacrifice to defend it and those for whom family needs took priority.

Responses to this open-ended question ranged from strong phrases of support for labor unions (e.g., that workers without unions are "mere slaves") to statements that unions are full of troublemakers and create more problems than they solve. More than one-third of the respondents (827, or 37 percent) said that they would reject the hypothetical job offer under the stated conditions; fewer than two-thirds (63 percent) said that they would accept it. Five percent said that they would first accept the employer's conditions and later join the union. Attitudes toward labor unions, and thus the value placed on ties among workers, varied widely.

In chapter 5 we saw that perceptions of the state were important in local political culture. Radical activists saw the state as antagonistic to the poor; they viewed struggle *(lucha)* as the most appropriate strategy for extracting concessions from Peru's central government. Clientelists saw the state as a benefactor of the poor; they turned to negotiations to secure assistance and services from the government. Two separate survey questions were designed to probe voters' understanding of their relationship to the state. First they were asked whether organizations in their neighborhood should be sponsored by the national government;[1] later they were asked the more strategy-related question whether "struggle" *(medidas de lucha)* or "legal petitioning" *(trámites legales)* was the better method for dealing with the state.

Responses to both questions reflect, again, considerable range in local opinion. About two-thirds of respondents (861, or 64 percent) favored national government sponsorship of local organizations, and about one-third (36 percent) opposed it. Similarly, 66 percent, or 787, said that legal petitioning was the better method for securing benefits for their community; 33 percent preferred "struggle."

Aggregate responses to each question indicate that Independencia's mass voting population appeared to hold alternatively "radical" and "clientelist" views of the state, fellow workers, and political strategy. But what evidence do we find of *patterns* of attitudes, of distinct political subcultures? A first step toward answering this question is to examine how likely it is that a person offering a "radical" response to one question will offer a similarly "radical" response to another question. Table 4 compares responses to the question "Is legal petitioning or struggle better?" among those who accepted and those who rejected the hypothetical job offer barring union affiliation. Responses to the two questions were associated, and in the predicted direction: those who demonstrated less support for labor unions, and thus less class consciousness, were significantly more likely to favor legal petitioning over "struggle" tactics, while those who rejected the job offer tended to prefer struggle over petitioning (the association is significant at the $p = .001$ level). Hence, with regard to these two questions at least, "radical" and "clientelist" views are clustered among Independencia's general voting population.

There was a similar clustering of opinion with regard to strategic preferences (struggle versus petitioning) and views of the state. As table 5 shows, those who favored legal petitioning also believed, at a

TABLE 4. Union Solidarity and Strategy Preference

Better strategy	Job without union affiliation?	
	Accept Job (%)	Reject Job (%)
Petition	71	59
Struggle	29	41
TOTAL	100	100
	($N = 462$)	($N = 284$)

$\chi^2 = 11.2$
$p < .001$

rate of more than two to one, that the state was an appropriate sponsor of organizations in their neighborhoods, whereas those who favored "struggle" were nearly evenly split on the question of state sponsorship (the association is significant at the $p = .001$ level). These results echo findings in the previous chapter: a preference for confrontation over negotiation is linked to a more general, sometimes visceral, mistrust of the state. Similarly, voters' views on the appropriateness of the relationship between the state and popular organizations are good predictors of their views on union solidarity: those who were wary of government sponsorship were significantly less likely to accept the hypothetical job offer, and those who favored state sponsorship were less likely to reject it (the association was significant at the $p = .05$ level).[2]

The answer, then, to our first question—was the bifurcated political culture of activists echoed in the district's mass electorate?—is a qualified yes. Certainly many people held views that from the perspective of the clientelist-radical dichotomy appear contradictory. Still, the data demonstrate a significant tendency for respondents to hold patterns of opinion consistent with the clientelist-radical dichotomy: an inclination toward *lucha* tends to accompany strong worker solidarity and suspicion of the state; an inclination toward conciliatory strategies tends to accompany weaker worker identifi-

TABLE 5.   Views of the Government and Strategy Preference

Better strategy	Should organizations in your neighborhood be sponsored by the government?	
	Yes (%)	No (%)
Petition	73	56
Struggle	27	44
TOTAL	100	100
	(N = 500)	(N = 280)

$\chi^2 = 23$
$p < .001$

cation and a preference for state sponsorship. This finding allows us to eliminate an alternative hypothesis that the shantytown population was a politically undifferentiated mass, using "radicalized" or "clientelistic" strategies pragmatically in response to the needs of the moment.

To put the point slightly differently, in chapter 5 I argued that participating in a clientelist or radical subculture made certain strategies unavailable to actors, because using these strategies would force them to violate their sense of identity or would undermine their authority in the community. The existence of competing patterns of opinion among the mass electorate in which preferences for strategies vary with other threads in the web of worldviews supports this notion that subcultures enable actors to use some strategies but make others unavailable to them.

We may proceed, then, to look for answers to the second set of questions. What social, demographic, and other contextual factors are associated with alternatively radical and clientelist patterns of political culture? A combination of factor and regression analysis helps to answer this question. Using principal-component analysis, a form of statistical analysis designed to discern common factors in several different variables, I reduced the three interrelated attitudinal variables—responses to the questions "Would you accept a job offer barring union affiliation?" "Is legal petitioning or struggle more effective?" and "Should organizations in your neighborhood be sponsored by the national government?"—to a single underlying factor.

Attitudinal variables	Loading of component factors on radicalism
Strategies	0.718
Views of the state	0.670
Class solidarity	0.524

Factor analysis confirmed that these three attitudinal variables could be seen as related to a single underlying concept or factor, degrees of radicalism.[3] Factor analysis had the additional advantage of providing factor loadings, which could then be used to score individual responses on a summary index of radicalism. Each respondent's answer to the three individual attitudinal questions could be weighted by the value given to produce an overall score for each individual on the underlying factor radicalism.

I then treated this underlying factor as the dependent variable in a multiple-regression model. I included in this model independent variables measuring the degree to which individual respondents were exposed to the sorts of changes that, according to the preceding historical analysis, were associated with the emergence of new social movements: exposure to labor unions, to radicalizing outside actors in local organizations, and to the "critical idea" that came to dominate the schools.

I also explored the impact of variables that would confirm hypotheses at odds with mine. Did men see the world around them differently than women did? Were young people prone to radicalism, older people to clientelism? Was the worldview of a person born in the city different from that of a person born in the *sierra*? Were people living in the lower, more established parts of the district inclined toward clientelism, those in the more squalid hillsides toward radicalism? Did any systematic differences appear between the industrial proletariat and service workers or workers in the informal sector? A positive answer to any of these questions would cast doubt on the notion that the split between radicals and clients reflected exposure to the organizations and experiences that since the Velasco years had produced alternatively combative and clientelist styles of political action.

The results of this analysis are shown in table 6. Differences in income or occupation, between people living in the "low" and "high" parts of Independencia, or between the young and the old were not significantly associated with attitudinal differences among Independencia's voters; political attitudes were influenced, however, by some exposure to labor unions, some involvement with certain local organizations, and a certain level of schooling.

Unions and political culture. People who either had joined a union at some time in their work life or had a spouse who was a union member scored higher on the index of radicalism than those with no such exposure. This effect is not an artifact of occupational differences: occupation, recorded by categories such as factory worker, service worker, informal-sector worker, or low-level white-collar employee, had no direct effect on political attitudes.[4] Thus if two people had similar occupations (and other characteristics in common) but one became involved in a union and the other did not, then the union member would tend to be the more radicalized of the two.[5]

Education and political culture. The direct relation between education and radicalism again confirms the role of changes initiated under Velasco in reshaping popular political culture. Classrooms in lower-class districts like Independencia's became a source of a newly critical consciousness, the result both of the Velasco curricular and pedagogical reforms and of Marxist parties' new sway over elementary and secondary teachers who joined SUTEP, the teachers' union. To some readers it may not seem surprising that higher educational achievement among *pobladores* should be associated with a more self-confident and confrontational approach to political strategy, a less dependent orientation toward the state, and heightened class consciousness. But recall that education played an important role in forming workers' political consciousness earlier in the century, when "social etiquette" manuals were employed to instill a sense of deference (see chapter 2).

Gender, participation, and political culture. Among the most significant changes that occurred in Peru during the 1970s and 1980s was the politicizing of gender, the entrance of the domestic and social

TABLE 6.   Results of Regression Analysis of Levels of Radicalism

Variable	DF	Parameter Estimate	Standard Error	T-Statistic	$p < T$	Standardized Estimate
Intercept	1	−0.696	0.241	−2.895	0.039	0
Unionism	1	0.485	0.123	3.929	0.000	0.152
Male participation[a]	1	0.368	0.117	3.131	0.002	0.122
Education[b]	1	0.099	0.041	2.423	0.016	0.106
Occupation[c]	1	0.070	0.089	0.784	0.433	0.031
Migrant[d]	1	0.020	0.099	0.201	0.841	0.009
Income	1	0.008	0.017	0.489	0.625	0.019

[a]Interaction term; see related discussion in the text.

[b]Measured according to the educational level the respondent achieved (i.e., none, some primary, primary school completed, some secondary, etc.).

[c]Measured as factory worker versus independent, service, or technical worker. Neither this nor alternative categorization of workers produced a statistically significant association.

[d]Scored as a dichotomous variable: migrant = 1, Lima native = 0. Neither length of residence in Lima nor a migrant's region of origin produced significant associations. The analysis of variance was as follows:

Source	DF	Sum of Squares	Mean Square	F Value	Prob > F
Model	6	46.549	7.758	6.356	0.0001
Error	658	803.193	1.221	—	—
TOTAL	664	849.543	—	—	—
R-square:	.0548	—	—	—	—
Adjusted R-square:	.0462	—	—	—	—

NOTE: Age has been omitted from the model because it is highly (negatively) correlated with education. Similarly, gender has been omitted because it is a component of, and thus highly correlated with, male participation. When age is entered into the model its beta estimate is -0.050 (standardized estimate -0.055); the probability of nonassociation of the related T-statistic is .281. When gender enters the model (scored as female = 0, male = 1), the beta estimate is .068 (standardized estimate .030) and the probability of nonassociation is .519.

A word should be said about the low value of the R-squared statistic associated with this regression model. Low coefficients of determination are endemic to cross-sectional survey analysis, as opposed to time-series and aggregate data analysis. It is my feeling that the low R-squared statistic in this context reflects, not a specification error, but other problems linked with survey research in a context like this one. The independent variables included in the model are clearly relevant to explaining variation in the dependent variable, as the T-statistics associated with their betas indicate.

TABLE 7. Union Solidarity and Gender

| | Would you accept a job barring union affiliation? | |
	Men	Women
Accept	56%	67%
Reject	44%	33%
TOTAL	100%	100%
	(N = 405)	(N = 391)

$p = .001$

conditions affecting women into the realm of political debate. Women also entered public affairs, national and local, in greater numbers than ever before. Women emerged as central actors in Peru's social movements, and not only in explicitly feminist organizations. Independencia offers many examples of the women who, under various influences, became vocal and visible activists.

Survey data confirm that gender affected the way a person saw class, strategy, and the state. But these data also force us to modify the impression we may have gotten in chapter 5 of women as more deeply imbued with the new ethic of participation and *lucha*. Instead these data suggest that many women, at least when compared with their male neighbors, remained somewhat more deferential to outside authorities and placed a lower value on class bonds.[6]

The data in table 7 demonstrate that when women were faced with the hypothetical dilemma of choosing between unemployment, on the one hand, and employment in a factory in which they were barred from joining the union, on the other, they were significantly more likely than men to chose employment. But such associations were much weaker between gender and responses to the other attitudinal questions. Indeed, when I explored the relation between gender and political radicalism, I found no significant association.

To explore further the relationship of gender, participation, and political radicalism, I constructed the variable "male participation," the third variable in table 6. "Male participation" is an interaction term that combines high meeting attendance with gender: men who reported attending two or more meetings a week were scored 1 on this dichotomous variable; women and less active men were scored 0. Active men were significantly more radicalized than inactive men, and they were more radicalized than women, whether the latter were active or not.

When men in Independencia joined organizations or movements, the experience politicized them: they placed greater importance on bonds among workers, and they acquired a propensity for *lucha* and an antagonism toward the state, all of which were missing in men who did not take part in community affairs. Women who joined organizations or movements did not generally undergo a similar change in worldview. Thus, barring other kinds of experiences (extensive schooling, involvement in labor unions), women—both the active and the inactive—resembled inactive men.

This finding also points toward a gap between a small group of women who were the embodiment of Peru's new, radicalized urban social movements—people like Esther Moreno, Independencia's mayor (1983–89), or Julia Romero, the washerwoman who relished taking on the local representatives of the military regime—and Clara Mayta, the Villa El Angel resident who thought of the neighborhood committee members as a natural elite, or Virginia Verdera, who yearned for a priest to give her a Christmas fruitcake. Women like Moreno and Romero were extremely visible, playing critical roles in the political life of the district; Mayta and Verdera were more typical of Independencia's women.

How can we interpret this finding? One explanation is that girls were socialized in a passivity and respect for authority that persisted later in life. If boys were taught deference early but internalized it less fully, such deference would be more easily neutralized by the experience of joining neighborhood committees or political parties.

We can also think about the relationship between community activism and political attitudes the other way around: just as some people's worldviews changed because of their organizational involvement (recall the words of Lidia García and Rosario Huayta in chapter 5), preexisting differences in worldview produce different reactions to community organizations. Men who think of the state as an antagonist, value class-solidary action, and think that staging noisy marches outside ministries is the way to get things done may predictably join organizations and movements in larger numbers than men who favor a less confrontational politics. Our data may indicate that women's motives in joining organizations were different from men's. Perhaps the possibility of getting a cheap meal for their children from the "popular dining hall" or of getting work through connections in a parish-run mothers' club was a more common stimulus for community involvement for the average shantytown woman.

Migrants, region, and political culture. Peru is a multiethnic society in which racial and class distinctions overlap with each other and with distinctions in regional origin. The shantytowns of Lima are microcosms of this racial, ethnic, linguistic, and regional diversity. Any given neighborhood in Independencia included many who were bilingual, speakers of Quechua and Spanish or of Aymara and Spanish, but many fewer who spoke only a native languages. According to the survey results, one-quarter of Independencia's population spoke some Quechua, Peru's predominant native language. Any given neighborhood also included many migrants from other regions, especially *serranos*, migrants from the Andean provinces (see table 8), and might also be home to a sprinkling of residents of African heritage, as well as to migrants from the northern or southern coast and the Amazon.

The cultural impact of the waves of migrants from the provinces is palpable in Lima and has been the subject of numerous studies.[7] Furthermore, several studies in Latin America have shown that being a migrant shapes the new lower-class city-dweller's political identity. Studies have also found differences in the social aspirations and hence political mood of migrants compared with their city-born offspring.[8] It is thus startling that these background factors played so small a part in framing the contemporary views of Independencia's residents. No significant differences in attitudes toward the state, strategy, and class appeared, for instance, between monolingual Spanish speakers and speakers of a native language. Nor did differences of any note appear between natives of Lima and migrants or between migrants from distinct regions of the country.

TABLE 8. Place of Birth of Independencia's Residents

Region	Percentage of Whole
Lima	38.8
Central highlands	23.2
Southern highlands	16.7
Northern coast	10.8
Northern highlands	6.1
Southern coast	2.5
Amazonian basin	1.9
TOTAL	100.0
	(N = 876)

These findings do not discount subtle differences among these groups. A shantytown dweller whose first language is Quechua must certainly experience the surrounding world of Lima in a way that differs from the way his or her thoroughly urbanized and monolingual Spanish-speaking neighbors do. It is equally certain that a relatively dark-skinned shantytown resident will face greater obstacles than a relatively light-skinned neighbor faces and adopt strategies that are distinct from those the latter adopts.[9] The survey findings do suggest, rather, that these differences were swamped by the powerful forces of political-cultural transformation unleashed under military rule. Because of these recent historical changes, political experiences, in particular whether and how often people came into contact with labor unions, schools, and local organizations, became much more important in molding popular political culture than language or place of birth.

The rise of a newly radicalized social movement is a phenomenon not of leaders and activists alone but of the broader population as well. People do not shift from one current to the other simply with advancing age; nor do these distinct currents reflect only occupational or income differences or differences between migrants and their offspring. Nor, finally, do distinct worldviews reflect the raw, unmediated effect of occupational differences: exposure to labor unions,

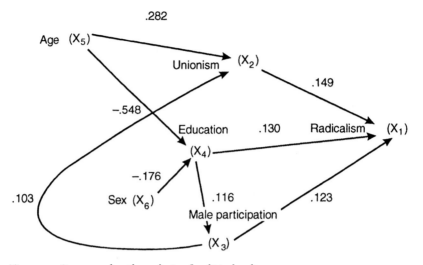

Figure 2. Compound path analysis of political culture

rather than differences in occupation, had a significant impact on the way Independencia's voters saw their surrounding world.

But what of the interrelations and causal chains among the various factors? We saw, for example, that higher educational levels are associated with class consciousness and strategic radicalism, whereas gender is not. But are not men and women likely to achieve different levels of education? Similarly, whereas we may be convinced that participation in local organizations is associated (among men) with a more confrontational consciousness, might not participation also affect Independencia's *pobladores* in other ways that in turn reinforce a more radicalized worldview?

Compound path analysis, presented in figure 2, offers a fuller understanding of the characteristics and life experiences of Independencia's residents and their effect on political consciousness.[10] Several aspects of the results illustrated in figure 2 merit emphasis.[11] Some of the primary factors were more powerful than originally envisioned, because they acted both directly and indirectly on the individual's political worldview. This was true both of male participation and of education: men who were active participants in local organizations were radicalized, and they also were more likely to join labor unions, which reinforced this shift in political worldview.[12]

Similarly, more schooling was tied to greater radicalism; it also left the individual more open to taking part in local organizations and in unions, again reinforcing the shift toward a radicalized worldview.[13]

These data clarify the impact of demographic and life-cycle variables on political orientation. Earlier I showed that the effect on political consciousness of joining organizations was different among men and women: men became more radicalized; women generally did not. Being male in Independencia also had a direct and strong effect on one's schooling: boys were more likely than girls to reach the upper grades and even to receive some postsecondary education, a difference that increased the combativeness of Independencia's active men in comparison with women, active or not.[14]

Path analysis also permits a fuller understanding of the impact of age on attitudes. We saw earlier that age had no independent effect, refuting the life-cycle hypothesis that today's radicals are tomorrow's clients. But age had a strongly negative association with education: the young were likely to receive many more years of schooling than were the old. This finding reflected the increased access of the poor to education, especially postsecondary education, since the Velasco reforms.[15]

Political Culture and Voting Behavior

In chapter 3 I cited two changes in lower-class voting behavior between the periods before and after military rule as evidence of a shift away from a clientelist political culture. Both changes were visible in ecological data. After military rule, for the first time the voters in lower-class districts voted differently from voters in higher-class districts. And there was a qualitative shift in the kind of candidates and parties that did well in poor districts, away from conservatives and toward populists and socialists.

The results of my survey allow us to explore these changes at the level of the individual shantytown voter. The survey provided ample information on individuals' voting behavior and thus an opportunity to examine the effect on voting behavior of political culture as well as demographic, socioeconomic, and experiential factors. The data shed light on the surprising rise of the electoral Left in Peru in the

1980s, a subject that has been taken up in ecological studies using aggregate results from electoral districts. Dietz's work explored the changing relationship between social class and party preference and the rise of class-based voting after the years of military rule.[16] The results of my study allow us to explore differences in voting behavior among the lower classes at the level of the individual voter and to isolate more precisely the factors that led them to support the Left as well as centrist and conservative parties.

One word of caution is in order before turning to the survey results: the survey results do not disclose how respondents actually voted, but only how, in May and June 1986, they remembered having voted in elections between 1980 and 1985. We can be sure there is not an exact correspondence between memory and vote, and the farther the election in question recedes into the past, the less reliable memory becomes. These data reflect, not the real historical evolution of preferences in voting, but the patterns of preference imposed on past voting, although this latter sort of information is itself relevant to the meaning of electoral choice.

One may wonder what voting means to people in a Third World shantytown. Do voters display any substantial stability of party preference from one election to the next, or do they shift randomly from one party to another? When they do shift votes (the macrolevel evidence shows that many did), are these changes focused on a Left-Center-Right dimension, or does such a dimension have little meaning for voters?

In fact the stability of party preference among Independencia's voters and the unidirectionality of changes in preference are striking. Respondents who reported having changed their party preference between the 1980 and 1983 Lima municipal elections, for example, shifted almost exclusively left. This unidirectionality is visible in table 9, which cross-tabulates party preference, simplified as a Left-Center-Right trichotomy, in these two elections.[17] An overwhelming majority (77 percent) is located on the main descending diagonal, having chosen the same party in both elections. What is more important, of the 123 respondents who reported having changed their party preference between the two elections, a full 84 percent clustered in the three cells to the right of the diagonal (corner *a*). Had this not been

TABLE 9. Party Choice in Municipal Elections, 1980 and 1983

1980 Election	1983 Election			
	Right	Center	Left	TOTAL
				(a)
Right	45	14	76	135
Center	2	165	13	180
Left	7	11	191	209
(b)				
TOTAL	54	190	280	

$$\frac{a}{a+b} = .84$$

the case—had similar numbers of voters shifted leftward and right-ward (meaning that the two off-diagonal corners would have had similar numbers of voters)—the Right-Center-Left positioning of voters would have been reshuffled, and the results would have cast doubt on the meaningfulness of a Right-Center-Left dimension for Independencia's voters.

The unidirectionality of change diminishes somewhat in comparisons between the presidential election of 1985 and other elections (see table 10). If we compare electoral choice in 1985 municipal elections with that in 1983, for example, we see that 63 percent of voters who changed their party choice shifted leftward, and 37 percent rightward. In 1985 APRA's campaign rhetoric stressed the party's anti-imperialist and labor-oriented tradition, while Alfonso Barrantes, the United Left's presidential candidate, stepped back from some of his promises, such as to nationalize industry and pursue workers' control of firms. The general view, shared by national political analysts as well as residents of Independencia, was that the ideological differences between APRA and IU narrowed.[18] Therefore, the bidirectionality of change between these two elections probably reflects a lessening of differences between APRA and the

TABLE 10.   Percentage of Respondents Changing Vote
Who Changed "against the Tide"

	1980 municipal	*1983 municipal*	*1985 presidential*	*1986 municipal*[a]
1980 presidential	13	3	3	2
1980 municipal		16	35	29
1983 municipal			21	37
1985 presidential				15

NOTE: Most voters who changed their vote between the 1980 presidential elections and the municipal elections of that year shifted leftward; those who shifted rightward made up only 13 percent of those who shifted. Reported percentages are calculated in the following way:

$$\frac{a}{a+b} \times 100$$

(see table 9).

[a]Respondents' anticipated party preference in the then upcoming municipal elections (November 1986).

United Left rather than a reshuffling of the electorate that was not ideologically informed.

That Independencia's voters arrayed themselves fairly consistently along a Right-Left continuum gives us confidence to view voting as an ideologically meaningful behavior. To explore what lay behind the surprising rise of the electoral Left in the 1980s (a shift presumably related to the growth of social movements and a radicalized political worldview), I constructed a scale of leftist voting. I did so by first ordering four elections (1980 presidential, 1980 municipal, 1983 municipal, and 1985 presidential) according to the percentage of votes cast for the Left in each election. The resulting ordering of elections appears in table 11.

In an election in which many people voted for the Left, it was in a sense relatively easy to support the Left: it required less of a firm commitment to leftist parties than in an election in which most people supported other parties. Each respondent was assigned a score depending on his or her pattern of support for the Left in the four elections: 1 for those who never voted for the Left; 2 for those who voted for the Left only in the 1983 municipal elections (when it was

TABLE 11.　Reported Support for the Left
in Four Elections

Election	Voters Reporting Support for the Left (%)
1983 municipal	51
1980 municipal	43
1985 presidential	29
1980 presidential	23

"easiest" to do so); 3 for those who voted for the Left in the 1983 municipal elections as well as the 1985 presidential elections (when it was "harder" to do so); 4 for those who voted for the Left in the 1983 municipal elections, the 1985 presidential elections, and the 1980 municipal elections; and 5 for those who voted for the Left in all four elections (see table 12).[19] (This measure had the disadvantage of requiring respondents to have voted in elections since May 1980 and thus excluded one-third of the sample's younger voters. I therefore complemented it with an analysis of voting patterns in the 1985 presidential elections alone.)

I then constructed a multivariate regression model to explain support for the Left, using the five-level scale of Left voting as the dependent variable. The results of that analysis, found in table 13, show that economic, participatory, and political-cultural factors each explained some variation in support for the Left.

The results of regression analysis are significant in that they show that attitudinal radicalism is associated with support for the electoral Left. The first independent variable in the regression model, radicalism, is a measure of commitment to the complex of attitudes that includes class solidarity, strategies of struggle, and antipathy toward the state, derived from my earlier factor analysis (see above). The finding suggests that the new electoral success of the Left in the 1980s was related to its ability to capture support from segments of the shantytown population who had become radicalized (in the sense used in chapter 5).

TABLE 12. Scores on a Scale of Left Voting Assigned
to Distinct Voting Patterns

Pattern of Left Voting	Score
Never	1
1983 municipal	2
1983 municipal and 1980 municipal	3
1983 municipal, 1980 municipal, and 1985 presidential	4
Always	5

TABLE 13. Regression Analysis of Voting Behavior

Variable	DF	Parameter estimate	Standard error	T-statistic	p < T	Standardized estimate
Intercept	1	3.184	.517	6.160	.0001	
Radicalism	1	0.167	.067	2.489	.0132	0.120
Income	1	0.065	.031	2.115	.0350	0.103
Female participation[a]	1	−0.549	.248	−2.212	.0112	−0.112

NOTE: The dependent variable is the propensity of voters to support the electoral Left in four elections. The analysis of variance is as follows:

Source	DF	Sum of Squares	Mean Square	F Value	p > F
Model	9	62.93	6.99	2.855	0.0029
Error	438	1072.75	2.45		
TOTAL	447	1135.68			

R-square: .0554
Adjusted R-square: .0360
[a]Dichotomous variable: active women scored 1; inactive women and men scored 0.

TABLE 14.   Political Orientation and Electoral Choice
in the 1985 Presidential Elections

| | Score on index of radicalism[a] | | | |
	Least	—	—	Most (%)
APRA	79	69	61	41
United Left	21	31	39	59
TOTAL	100	100	100	100
	(N = 188)	(N = 242)	(N = 140)	(N = 56)

[a]Factor loadings for each of the three component variables generated in the factor analysis mentioned earlier were used to construct this index. Each respondent was assigned a score of 0 (for a "clientelist" answer) or 1 (for a "radical" answer) to each of the three component attitudinal questions. These responses, weighted by the factor loading for each of the three variables, was then summed to produce a final score in which eight discrete values were possible. Here the middle six scores are collapsed into two columns. The range of scores in the second column is .524 to .718; the range in the third column is 1.194 to 1.342.

$\chi^2 = 31.3$
$p < .001$

Further evidence of this association between voting behavior and political worldview comes from cross-tabulations of voting behavior in the 1985 presidential elections and respondents' levels of radicalism (see table 14).[20] For Peru's urban poor, the 1985 presidential elections amounted to a two-way race between APRA's Alan García and the United Left's Alfonso Barrantes (very few shantytown dwellers in Independencia or elsewhere supported the candidate of a coalition of rightist parties). Table 14 shows that support for the Left in this election was directly related to attitudinal radicalism. The relationship is monotonic, with each successive increase in level of radicalism associated with rising support for the United Left and declining support for APRA. As significant segments of the urban poor were radicalized in the 1980s, that radicalization was successfully harnessed by the Left and converted into electoral support for United Left candidates.

In addition to political worldview, other factors help account for electoral support. In contrast to what was revealed by our analysis of factors shaping worldviews, economic differences were relevant to differences in voting behavior. Respondents to the survey reported annual household incomes ranging from about $70 to about $2,500; the average annual income was $350 per household. Among the approximately 80 percent of respondents reporting an annual household income below $375 per year, support for the Left increased with income; above that level the trend leveled off and was to some degree reversed. Although self-reported income should be treated with caution, nevertheless, the increased support for the Left among the middle-income stratum in this generally poor community is provocative. Perhaps it reveals a greater tendency of the very poor to support more traditional conservative or populist parties, in contrast to a stronger propensity among those in the middle, who are still by any objective standard poor but who possess some greater security, to vote in a manner that reflects greater independence from parties that traditionally cultivated ties of dependence with squatters. We can imagine a desperately poor family turning to the Popular Christian Party–sponsored family dining hall mentioned in chapter 3, which opened two weeks before the 1985 presidential election and disappeared days later. Such a family might have voted for the PPC out of a sense of either gratitude or obligation. It is tempting, finally, to think of residents in the highest income groups as voting for more conservative parties and politicians because of a class identification with them (the kind of identification that the clientelists of chapter 5 indeed showed). But the failure of our attitudinal variable to vary systematically with income works against this hypothesis.

Survey results throw further light on the different ways men and women were socialized to political life in Independencia. The earlier discussion suggested that men who took an active part in community organizational life were radicalized. It is now clear that this radicalizing in turn led them to support left-wing candidates. It is also clear that a changed political worldview was the mechanism that led men to support the Left, because at any given level of attitudinal radicalism male participation had no independent impact on voting behavior. Among women, on the other hand, joining local organizations had no impact on patterns of consciousness (see above). Furthermore, women who took an active part in local organizations, no matter what their previous level of attitudinal radicalism, became *less* likely to support leftist candidates.

The finding is surprising. Perhaps the explanation lies in differences between the kinds of organizations men and women tended to join. We saw in chapter 3 that neighborhood committees, church-sponsored organizations, and political parties had mixed and unpredictable relations with their members. Church workers seemed particularly likely to evolve into brokers between the community and the outside benefactors, even when they themselves wished to distance themselves from what they disparagingly called assistentialism. My field experience uncovered strong feelings among church operatives of competing with leadership training centers, non-church women's clubs, and the municipal government, all of which were tied to the Left. These tensions persisted despite the considerable overlap in ideological (or theological) perspectives of the two sets of actors, the socialist Left and the liberation theology–inspired church. The tension seemed tied to nuns' and lay workers' view that active community residents ought to be involved exclusively in church activities. Perhaps this perspective derived from the religious workers' sense that they were trying to construct a community of God in the shantytown, not just provide services and make improvements: this community should be all-absorbing, and "sharing" activists was incompatible with this desire for a new community. Thus, the fact that many more women than men were active in church organizations could explain the tendency of activism to make women more hostile to the Left:[21] the nuns and lay workers whose influence they came under may have communicated to them their hostility toward the local secular leftists, leading women to vote against the Left more frequently than their male counterparts. This despite an affinity, indeed a kind of implicit alliance, between the socially oriented church and the partisan Left in national politics.

Compound path analysis allows us to detect the full impact of attitudinal, economic, and demographic variables on voting behavior, discerning indirect associations between variables mediated through third variables (see fig. 3).[22] Education again emerges as central to producing support for the Left. Higher levels of education were associated with a more radicalized political worldview, which in turn

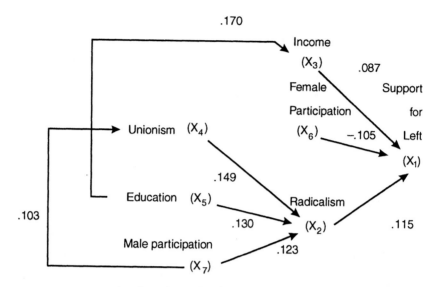

Figure 3. Compound path analysis of Left voting

produced greater support for candidates of the Left; education also raised incomes, and higher incomes were also associated with greater support for the Left.

How does this analysis sharpen the understanding imparted by earlier studies of macropolitical changes in Peru, in particular the emergence of massive lower-class support for the Left and hence the Left's electoral victories of the 1980s? In explaining the rise of working-class support for the Left, Dietz pointed to a number of macrolevel factors, such as changes in national economic conditions, the fluidity of the Peruvian party system, and variation in the goals and meanings of elections, such as between local and national elections.[23] The recent history of elections in Independencia supports some of these findings. Local elections always produced a greater leftist vote than did national elections. But we can now answer an additional question, namely, Given the overall shift toward support for the electoral Left in the 1980s, what were the individual-level experiences that "made" leftist voters and distinguished them from centrist and rightist voters, who continued to make up a large proportion of working-class Lima? This question leads us to focus on factors not discussed by Dietz, such as education and particular patterns of involvement with community organizations.

General Conclusions

What general points can we carry away from the preceding analysis? The first is that a political-cultural rift existed in Independencia. Specific historical factors, rather than enduring structural or life-cycle factors, produced this rift: radical voters were distinguished from their clientelist neighbors by their greater exposure to labor unions and their more extensive schooling. The qualities of the labor movement and the educational system that could be expected to be associated with lower-class radicalism were initiated in Peru in the 1970s under the Velasco military government. None of the other sources of difference in the shantytown population—levels of acculturation to urban mestizo culture, place of birth, period of or age at migration, residential zone within the shantytown, or occupation—had a significant impact on political consciousness or voting behavior. Similarly lacking in influence were factors tied to age. Instead the radicalized political subculture was the result of specific recent historical changes affecting the political life of the shantytowns.

The community's organizational life reproduces both confrontational and clientelist mentalities, and both leftist and center-or-rightist voting. Community organizations did not uniformly give rise to a protest politics; rather, certain kinds of organizations (those commonly joined by men) shaped their members into class-conscious and combative actors, whereas others (those commonly joined by women) had no effect on political worldview and produced more conservative voters.

Finally, combative and class-conscious views and practices among shantytown dwellers represented more than a different strategy for achieving traditional goals. We saw that a preference for a confrontational style of activism was associated with a heightened sense of class solidarity and a generalized sense of antagonism toward the state. We also saw that support for the partisan Left was similarly—and strongly—dependent on a generally confrontational mentality.

This second point merits some reflection: the rapid and surprising rise of the Peruvian socialist Left as a force in electoral politics in the 1980s was associated with a fairly deep change in consciousness of the lower classes. Voting for the Left, like other nontraditional practices, was not simply a new electoral strategy to achieve traditional ends; the political ends of a substantial subset of Peru's lower classes had themselves been transformed.

Chapter 7

Social Movements,
Hegemony, and the State

What broader lessons do we learn from the Peruvian experience? The sequence of changes that produced a protest politics among Peru's urban poor was the following. A military leadership took state power and aspired to reconstitute state-society relations according to a corporatist design. For both ideological and strategic reasons, the leadership identified poor urban communities as a potential new base of support and attempted to activate these communities by building new organizational channels that would stimulate state-supportive mobilization. The military government sought support from the urban and rural lower strata at the same time that it took actions, such as land reform and changes in property rules in industry, that predictably alienated the elite that historically had constituted the social base of the Peruvian state.

But the military government was unsuccessful in remaking the social bases of state power. It was unable to remake the urban poor into a pillar of support. Instead, the urban poor bifurcated into relatively passive state clients on the one hand and unruly makers of social movements on the other. I turn now to the reasons why the Peruvian state's strategies for remaking the structure of lower-class interest representation failed and the theoretical implications of that failure.

Lower-Class Interest Representation in Peru: Clientelism and Corporatism

Clientelism. Clientelist relations between the state and the urban poor persisted, frustrating the military regime's project. That a dominant actor may be frustrated by the persistence of clientelism contradicts many accounts of this pattern of social interaction. Earlier I defined *clientelism* as a dyadic relation between two unequal actors in which the superior actor trades goods and services for other valued goods (political support, labor) from the inferior actor. Although the exchange is beneficial to both parties in some limited ways, it does not enhance the power of the inferior actor. Clientelism is thus a strategy for dominant groups to retain their position of superiority. That its persistence might actually run against the interests of a state elite is surprising and deserves some explanation.

Why did clientelism among the urban poor not shore up the Peruvian military government? A part of the answer may be that clientelism was an irritant to the military regime's more radical members, who saw the regime's goals as including a more profound empowerment of the lower classes: clientelist relations may have produced conflicts among state officials, undermining the internal unity of the regime. What is more important, the patron-client link between the state and the poor turned out not to be robust and failed to produce a following that would come to the defense of the regime when an alternative state leadership threatened it.

One can draw from this case the more general insight that patron-client ties are suited to reproducing well-established relations of domination and subservience but less effective as instruments of political change. The kind of exchange involved in patron-client ties is conserving, not transformative. Dominant actors (e.g., the Peruvian military government) that want not stability but a new basis of power are not well served by clientelism, at least not until new equilibria of social and political power relations are in place. In situations of flux the patron may have to call on clients for a more risky and heroic defense than the latter are predisposed to give. The early years of military rule in Peru, when the state leadership attempted to remake the social bases of its support, was just such a period of flux.

Corporatism. The Peruvian military regime unintentionally gave rise to two patterns of political relations: clientelism and social movements. But it failed to give rise to the pattern of political relations that it did set out to encourage: corporatism. What does Peru's failed corporatist project tell us more generally about state corporatism?

One lesson was suggested in chapter 3. The construction of a corporatist system of interest representation in a system previously characterized by some organizational pluralism requires eliminating all but one of the numerous organizations of a social group that compete to represent the group's interests. When this process of elimination is not reinforced with repression against the "loser" organizations, the agents of corporatist transformation are likely to create ready-made oppositions to themselves. This is a contradiction inherent in "inclusionary" (as opposed to "exclusionary") corporatist projects.[1] This is not to say that exclusionary or repressive corporatist regimes do not also create problems for themselves. The Peruvian case does, however, suggest contradictions in the strategy of rule of inclusionary corporatist regimes, contradictions that are likely to surface immediately.

A second lesson from this case of failed corporatism is that it is not accidental that in most successful efforts at installing corporatist systems, in Latin America and elsewhere, the labor movement is the state's interlocutor among the lower classes. Peru's military leadership shared with other architects of corporatism an instinct to turn for support to organized labor, but labor was already controlled by a political party of long standing (APRA). The regime therefore adopted a two-track strategy: severing the link between labor and its traditional party sponsor and turning to residentially defined communities of workers and the poor as an alternative corporatist base. The regime had only partial success in its strategy with labor: it was able to pry the labor movement away from its traditional party sponsors, but it was not able then to put itself in their place.

The state was left, then, with the second track of its strategy, which turned out to have serious limitations. Are there general reasons why geographical communities of poor people provide an unstable pillar for corporatist systems? In capitalist societies, functional groups such as labor unions represent workers who are by definition involved in ongoing exchange relations with the owners of capital, exchanging labor for wages. Both labor and capital require this exchange relation to continue if each is to survive; but the relation also engenders regular and predictable conflicts, mostly over the terms of the exchange. These conflicts in turn create an ongoing role for the state as intermediary. Corporatist regimes institutionalize this intermediary role in particular ways.

Lower-class organizations that grow out of geographically defined communities tied to consumption and reproduction do not create the same kinds of opportunities for state intervention. Demands made by these communities typically are not demands on third parties that the state can mediate but rather direct demands on the state itself. The community-state tie is also distinct from the labor-capital tie in that the former has less of the quality of mutual need than the latter. Capitalists need workers and therefore are forced to listen to their demands, although obviously such factors as the availability of an unused workforce and the level of unionization will influence the degree of employer responsiveness. Even in the most unpropitious circumstances for labor, however, owners usually are willing to engage in some form of negotiations over the terms of exchange with labor. This is not so in poor residential communities. The state, their main interlocutor, does not have to reproduce its relationship with squatters or shantytown dwellers for its own survival; or, perhaps more accurately, even if its ultimate political survival does depend on the support of these communities, the state does not view its dependence on them as ongoing or urgent.

The mixed and subtle, indeed contradictory, relationship between the state and lower-class communities during the early period of military rule in Peru illustrates the difficulties of creating the corporatist ties with nonproductive collectivities. The state's effort to cultivate Lima's shantytowns was halfhearted and incomplete. Drives to distribute land titles were lackadaisical and in communities like Independencia gave out before they had gone very far. The state tended to respond to needs and demands it invented for these communities rather than to demands that emanated from the communities themselves. State investment per person in the shantytowns was small compared with investments in wealthier areas. Because the state did not need the squatters in the same day-to-day way that employers need workers, its relationship with them was sporadic. And so, when the state leadership needed lower-class support, as when it was faced with a challenge from within for control over the state apparatus, that support was reluctantly given and shallow.

The failure of geographically based corporatism left the military regime unrooted in civil society. That this failure worked against the political interests of the state leadership is fairly obvious. A more complex question is whether it worked against the interests of the urban poor. Had the military's corporatist project been more successful, the result would have been, instead of the emergence of independent social movements, the construction of a politically and economically favored institutionalized mass base for the state. To judge whether this or the actual outcome would have better served the interests of the popular sectors, one would have to consider such questions as whether corporatist states with an initial populist thrust have incentives to continue to cultivate their popular-sector bases after lower-class support has become institutionalized. Examples to the contrary abound.

In reality, after the return to civilian rule, Peru's more mobilized popular sectors faced limited access to power, even under fairly open electoral systems and formally democratic institutional arrangements. The tepid responsiveness of the Peruvian state to the popular sectors under formally democratic institutional arrangements suggests that the rise of independent social movements was no guarantee of political empowerment or improved material welfare.

Social Movements and Hegemony in Peru

How useful, in the end, is the emphasis I have given throughout to the mentalities and consciousness of the makers of Peru's new urban social movements? To answer this question it is helpful to review the sequence of changes that have produced social movements in Peru, this time paying more attention to the micromechanisms involved.

The changes under military corporatist rule that set the stage for new lower-class movements may be summarized as a transformation of the settings in which Peru's urban poor were socialized to political life. The rise of the "classist" labor movement, the injection of the "critical idea" of Peruvian history and society into public school curricula, the arrival in the shantytowns of legions of outside organizers with new messages about the sources of poverty and possibilities for change—all of these, direct or indirect results of military government policies, transformed the worldviews of large segments of the urban poor. The new worldview appealed strongly to many poor people who lived in a society of extraordinary differences in income and wealth and in a political system that had been slow to respond even to very simple needs.

This scenario underscores difficulties in the macrostructural, rational-choice, and interest interpretations of lower-class resistance reviewed in chapter 1. The intentional, reflective quality of lower-class action and the changing lower-class consciousness over time demonstrate the limitations of Theda Skocpol's assumptions that lower-class actors are driven by macrostructural forces. But the implications of the study for rational choice and James Scott's interest theory are subtler.

Independencia and rationality. Studies of movements from below drawing on the insights of rational choice theory have frequently focused on the conditions that allow lower-class agents to overcome the free-rider problem (through mutual monitoring in small communities or through the extension of selective incentives by political entrepreneurs).[2] These may often be the key steps to collective action, but they were not crucial in the Peruvian case. It might be appealing to think of the outside organizers from the Catholic church, political parties, or the state as "political entrepreneurs" who extended selective incentives to shantytown dwellers. But the concept of political entrepreneurship would be misapplied here. The real story of political mobilization in Peru was not the extension of excludable material benefits or other selective incentives to actors who previously had withheld activism because they knew they could benefit from the activism of others.

In Independencia the event leading to mobilization was not the creation of organizations; organizations had always existed in the district. Rather, under military rule organizations emerged that promulgated an ethic of rights, protest, participation, and egalitarianism.

Other kinds of organizations also arose or persisted, organizations that emphasized personalism, deference, the benefits of control by a political elite, and the naturalness of hierarchies. These two kinds of organizations ordered the preferences and shaped the beliefs of their members in very different ways, creating different styles and patterns of collective action, or inaction.

Rational choice theorists define rational behavior as striving to attain desires by following optimal strategies based on beliefs that are sound given the information available. In this formulation, *desires* are the ends that people want, and *beliefs* are the understandings of the causal relation between courses of action and the results they yield. Actors can act irrationally in several senses. For example, they may act on irrational desires that conflict with their long-term happiness (they are thus *substantively* irrational); or they may act on irrational beliefs, flawed understandings of the relation between actions and their likely results (they are thus *cognitively* irrational).

Certainly there was a rational quality to the behavior of radicals and clientelists in Independencia: both strove to realize their normative vision of what social and political relations ought to be like, and they acted strategically to achieve those ends. But a deeper assessment of their desires and beliefs shows that political practice in the shantytown was not always rational. Intellectual domination was one source of "irrationality." Let us assume for the moment that the desires and beliefs of clientelists, and of many shantytown residents prior to military rule, were different from the desires and beliefs these actors would have developed had hegemonic influences not operated on them. That is, let us assume (as I will argue more fully below) that their desires and beliefs were not autonomous but imposed. And let us further assume that acting on these imposed desires and beliefs could be shown to further not their own interests but those of the dominant, interests that conflicted with their own. To the extent that this was true, clientelist action, even of a highly strategic sort, could be either substantively or cognitively irrational. It could produce results antithetical to those that the hypothetical autonomous actor would have preferred; or it could fail to produce the results they preferred because of (imposed) flawed beliefs about the best course of action to get what they wanted.

Let us consider, for example, the antipathy of some Independencia residents to labor unions. Two-thirds of the survey respondents said that if they were unemployed, they would accept a job offer contingent on their not joining a union. Many who said that they would accept such a job offer were undoubtedly pro-union, but not to the point of sacrificing employment. Some, however, offered expressly anti-union views, such as the assertion that unions are full of troublemakers. Among this subset of respondents were people like Reynaldo Rojas, industrial or service-sector workers who worked in heavily unionized industries but opposed unionization. Of course among such people we would find myriad reasons for opposition to unions. But we know that some of them opposed unions because unions violated the clientelists' social ideal: unions tended to flout norms of social decorum, replace individual supplication with group demands, and stress class solidarity over affinity among the lowly for the rich. Unions, in short, were the domain of the *resentidos*, the resentful ones, who had not learned to consent to social differences; in the clientelists' ideal society poor people accepted such social differences.

Labor unions tend to raise the wages of the employed; and it seems fair to assume that, left to their own devices, members of the Peruvian working class would prefer higher wages to lower ones. Unions may of course increase unemployment. But people like Reynaldo Rojas said they opposed unions not because they feared losing their jobs but because unions "create problems" and make "public" employer-worker dealings that should be personal and "direct" *(trato directo)*.

The conclusion that the prototypical Rojas's desires were substantively irrational would flow from the following assumptions: (1) that he desired both high wages and a peaceful, decorous hierarchical society; (2) that the source of his desire for high wages lay within himself, whereas the source of his desire for a peaceful hierarchical society lay in dominant institutions (and a good deal of evidence has been offered showing this to be true), that is, that were it not for hegemonic influence, he would desire high wages but not a peaceful, hierarchical society; (3) that his actions, in this case opposing unionization, reflected the priority of his (imposed) desire for social peace over his (autonomous) desire for higher wages (this preference ordering might itself reflect hegemonic influence); and (4) that his

opposition to unions frustrated is own long-term happiness (his happiness as he would judge it were he able to do so autonomously,
without hegemonic influence) by keeping his wages low.

Alternatively, hegemonic influence might be conceived as operating at the level of causal beliefs, producing behavior that is *cognitively
irrational*. Workers like Rojas might simply wish to maximize their
wages and might uncritically accept the belief that deference rather
than unions are the best route to achieving this goal. Suppose that
Rojas is faced with two kinds of information: direct knowledge of other
workers in his field who are unionized and, as a result of collective
bargaining, earn wages higher than his; and claims from employers
that one gets ahead in life by being polite and deferential. Deciding
which kind of information is better is not easy. And to the extent that
he has been inculcated with the view that conflict is bad, and deference
good, not instrumentally but normatively; to the extent that he feels
affinity with the wealthy and disdain for workers; in sum, to the extent
that he is immersed in clientelist culture, he may be biased against
evidence that unions raise wages. Again, by a narrow definition his
behavior may well be cognitively irrational, but given the power of
institutions that wish to lead him astray, it is easy to understand his
mistaken beliefs.[3]

Political action in Independencia demonstrates the limitations of
rationality in another way, related to the relative importance of strategic versus norm-driven behavior. Frequently I have described the
practices of actors in Independencia, such as street marches or one-
on-one meetings, as *strategies*, actions taken for instrumental reasons,
as efficient methods for achieving goals. I have described them, that
is, as actions that were strategically informed and not subject to
normative or other nonstrategic evaluations. But a careful reader of
chapter 5 will find this usage jarring, because so much "strategy" was
in fact informed by (conflicting) normative senses of right and wrong
methods of political action. The normative and the strategic com-
mingled in Independencia's political life in ways that defy easy sep-
aration. Radicals thought pressure tactics were the only effective way
of influencing a class state, but they also thought the "participation"
that pressure tactics involved was valuable in itself, the right way to
act, regardless of the consequences. Julia Romero's words aptly con-

vey this mix of strategic and normative orientations: "Whenever people have made demands . . . we have participated, we've supported them, we've even gone on marches with no reason so that people would realize that this is a place where people fight."

So closely was the positive normative evaluation—that x was the right thing to do—tied to the positive strategic judgment—that x was the efficient way to achieve y—that one suspects wishful thinking. Finding justice in actions that are initially adopted because they appear instrumentally efficient can redouble the actor's sense of having chosen the right course.[4] But the sequence in Independencia was frequently the reverse: the course initially chosen because it was consistent with the actor's normative views was then conveniently also judged to be strategically efficient. The difference is important. In the first case political action is shaped by a strategic, purposive orientation that is then dressed up by norms; in the second, political action is shaped by norms, conceptions of how one ought to act, and then these norm-driven actions are found to be strategically sound. I believe that the latter is the more faithful account of political action in Independencia.

Jon Elster places non-outcome-oriented actions in the category of norms. Not all norms are "normative" in the sense of being attached to a salient sense of right and wrong. Many are simply collective habits, or shared rules that actors are usually unaware of and could not even render if asked, just as the native speaker of a language can follow a rule of grammar without being able to render a statement of the rule. Rather than being guided by unconnected norms, Independencia's bifurcated patterns of political action formed two more or less coherent wholes, each encompassing both strongly and explicitly held right-and-wrong norms and unconscious collective habits. I prefer to think of these patterns as cultures (or subcultures, that is, of radicalism and clientelism), and the antagonistic actions they gave rise to as a manifestation of cultures in conflict.

Interest theory: the antinomies of James Scott. My questions in chapter 1 were formulated largely in response to James Scott, who believes that historians and social scientists who describe systems of domination as resting on hegemony start with false assumptions or use faulty methods, or both. Before using the Peruvian experience to answer my own questions, I turn to difficulties in Scott's own analysis of peasant resistance in Malaysia and in his theoretical considerations of hegemony. An extended critique is merited because Scott's work is masterful and influential and his conclusions differ from those contained in this study.

Scott's study of rural class relations in Malaysia is massive and subtle, but I will try to reduce it to its essentials. Rich peasants in the Kedah state of Malaysia had traditionally faced labor shortages at moments in the paddy production cycle, and had relied on a set of institutions—Islamic charity, public liberality, loans—to secure the loyalty of particular agricultural laborers and tenants. Changes in production after the Green Revolution in the early 1970s lessened the labor requirements in paddy production, making these institutions obsolete. Poor peasants tried to shame the rich into maintaining their charity and favors by appealing to norms of piousness and magnanimity. This was pure strategy, however, since the poor had never believed that the rich were pious or magnanimous but rather had understood these mechanisms of labor control for just what they were.

Scott reports that the poor directed a flow of derisive commentary and malicious gossip against the rich, which certainly convinces us that the poor peasants were not in the thrall of dominant ideology. But the decisive issue is whether the poor ever did believe that rich peasants treated them charitably because the rich were charitable people. If they did, then they confused practices of labor control with spontaneous generosity. About poor villagers' understanding of the setting of rents in the earlier period Scott says, "The attitude of landlords when rents were adjustable was described as magnanimous *(senang kira)*." As Amin, a poor villager, put it, "Before they said, 'if the harvest is bad, [we'll] reduce [the rent] a bit.' Then you could bargain, *there was compassion.* Now they only care about the money."[5] In a similar vein, poor peasants in Sedaka harked back to the old days of generosity and piousness on the part of the rich, in contrast to their stinginess and failure to "fear God" now. Scott sees this harking as a stratagem used by the poor to shame the rich into acting generously now. "This phenomenon of the 'good old days' is, of course, socially created for the explicit purpose of comparison with the current situation."[6] But Scott's claim that such forms were not *at that time* understood as

reflecting the authentic generosity of the rich remains only an assertion.[7]

If we accept at face value the poor villagers' frequent recollection
of earlier public liberality as reflecting the magnanimity of the rich,
then we have here a strong piece of evidence of hegemony. *Generosity, magnanimity, piousness*—at least in English these terms imply
inherent traits, not grudging behavior that one follows to serve a
material self-interest. If poor villagers thought of their rich neighbors
as unconditionally magnanimous *(senang kira),* not as magnanimous
only when they were threatened with labor shortages, then the poor
were wrong; indeed Scott's account proves them to have been wrong.
When the labor shortage disappeared, the magnanimity also largely
disappeared. "False consciousness" and "mystification" are heavy
labels to hang on this mistake. If my alternative reading of Scott's
material is right, then all the poor peasants did was make an error in
assessing the underlying motivations of the rich (an error that the rich
would have expended effort to lead them to make), and a hair-splitting
error at that: they failed to distinguish unconditional generosity from
generosity conditional on self-interest.[8]

The ability of the dominant class to assume intellectual and moral
leadership by claiming that their prominence flows from their concern
for the good of all, and the inability (in normal times) of the subordinate classes to transcend the linguistic and conceptual terms that the
dominant offer to explain their leadership, is Antonio Gramsci's most
basic understanding of hegemony.[9] Rich peasants who behave with
magnanimity because they have at heart the interests of all members
of the community are worthy of their position of power and authority;
rich peasants who behave magnanimously while doing so serves their
best interests have much more limited moral, intellectual, and political claims to authority.

Beyond the ambiguity of his own case material, there are other
reasons we should resist thinking that Scott has definitively disposed of the hegemony question. We should be troubled by the
all-inclusiveness of Scott's definitions of verbal and practical resistance, which threatens to make his propositions unfalsifiable. When
subalterns seem to express consent to their own domination, it is likely
that they are strategically feigning consent in order to make the system

work to their best advantage. He gives us little guidance regarding how we would know if they were not feigning. Scott leaves even less room for distinguishing when acts such as petty theft or foot-dragging constitute resistance, as he nearly always regards them to be, and when they are motivated by, for example, hunger or fatigue. It is wrong-headed, Scott thinks, to investigate the intentions lying behind these actions: the motives of actions of the lower classes seldom leave a trace in the historical record. Even when we are dealing with living people, we will look in vain for system-transformative intentions, even among those whose actions help bring on revolutions.

The omnipresent motive of the poor, Scott insists, is survival. When poor peasants deserted the army of the provisional government in Russia in the summer of 1917, they were not trying to bring that government down, much less bring about the new order envisioned by the Bolsheviks. They were instead tired of famine at the front and knew that land grabs were going on at home. These were not lofty revolutionary acts but "petty, self-interested acts of insubordination." According to Scott, "A peasant soldier who deserts the army is in effect 'saying' by his act that the purposes of this institution and the risks and hardships it entails will not prevail over his family or personal needs."[10] Is the peasant soldier who does not desert the army when others do saying that the purposes of the institution prevail over family or personal needs? This might be a logical conclusion, but one looks in vain in Scott's work for a sense of what true consent by the poor would look like.

Scott is obviously bent on vindicating the intelligence and capacity for creative action of the subordinate classes. Why, then, does he insist that survival is the only principle they can ever have in mind when acting politically, or, even more to the point, that when they appear to act "politically" they are just happening upon collective ways to defend their "survival"? We would do well to recall Gramsci's dictum that all men are philosophers. Survival is obviously an unassailable motive, and Scott is right to ridicule those who use terms like *self-indulgent* to describe the self-interested actions of the poor. I would defer to him on the political motives of the Southeast Asian peasantry, but he wants to extend his conclusions to all subordinate classes. When Josefina Ruiz sits in her shanty on a hillside above Lima and imagines "making this Peru a socialist Peru where there won't be bosses or exploiters," is she concerned only with "survival"? Even Julia Romero's conception of a "new society" where "we all eat or no one eats" is several steps removed from the survival instinct: she is imagining a society that allocates goods in a way that is radically different from that of the society in which she lives.[11]

One lesson from the Peruvian case is that changes in consciousness can explain new movements from below. Some lower-class actors came to hold new goals (e.g., they imagined new kinds of social orders and strove to make them actual); new beliefs (e.g., they thought raw pressure induced the state to act); and new identities (e.g., they behaved in conformity with a new image of themselves as poor people who fully participated in community affairs). Changed consciousness is not the sole or ultimate cause of Peru's new urban movements; this change has itself to be explained. But had these new goals, beliefs, and identities not appeared, *this* movement also would not have appeared. We know that because the neighbors of the movement makers, people who were sociologically similar to them but whose goals, beliefs, and identities remained unchanged, were not involved in the making of movements; in fact they resisted them because of their own opposed goals, beliefs, and identities.

In considering movements from below, Charles Tilly has written that "a sense of injustice is too pervasive, and rebellion too rare, for one to be a sufficient explanation of the other."[12] While a sense of injustice may be pervasive, it is not omnipresent; and grievances are not unchanging, either in level or in content: this is a second lesson from Peru. Poor people were exposed to a dominant ideology of personal dependence and acquiescence during the oligarchic state period, and that ideology in some measure "took." I use the phrase "dominant ideology," not in the sense that dominant ideas completely defined the worldview of the poor, but in the sense that this ideology emanated from the state, political parties, schools, and the church, all of which in that period more or less self-consciously used their influence among the poor to maintain social order. The counterhegemonic ideology, which the Peruvian state itself promoted during the period of military rule (granted with some ambivalence, and with results that went far beyond those intended), stressed participation, mobilization, and popular empowerment. The counterhegemonic ideology was central to undermining a culture of clientelism and deference, thus laying the cultural groundwork for a more rights-conscious and confrontational popular movement.

Peru's lower-class actors were not simply empty vessels into which alternative outside ideologies were poured. The dominant ideology, with its language of clientelism, left many experiences uninterpreted and many sentiments unexpressed; the ability of the counterhege-mony to interpret these experiences and express these sentiments more fully gave it power and appeal in poor neighborhoods like Independencia. The distinction between ideologies from "outside" and "inside" the shantytowns breaks down, furthermore, when we consider the impact on outside organizers of the perspectives and experiences of people in the lower-class communities where they went to work (and sometimes to live). Although my evidence is not sys-tematic, church workers, party organizers, and teachers working in the neighborhoods of Independencia often saw themselves as having been changed by coming to know a working-class community. The coun-terhegemonic ideology that grew out of the Velasco years is best seen as the product of an intermingling of the poor and the "outsiders," whose daily lives became intertwined.

Let me return now to the five questions laid out in the first chapter. *1. Does the consciousness of the subaltern classes replicate the dis-course of the dominant?* I have presented evidence throughout that indeed parts of the mental outlook, both normative and cognitive, of Peru's urban lower classes paralleled the discourse of the dominant. Much of the evidence of intellectual domination came from the analysis of the oligarchic state period, when dominant discourse was more successful in shaping the understandings and limiting the lan-guage of popular political culture than it was after the Velasco military years. We saw evidence of deference and fatalism in the lyrics of creole waltzes, a deference and fatalism that paralleled the messages that the Catholic Church emitted, such as that those who accepted their lowly status in this world would be exalted in the next. We saw evidence that working-class *aprista* union organizers accepted natural-hierarchy theories similar to those promulgated in "social etiquette" texts in the public schools, theories that led these unionists to insist that working-class party militants in APRA had to defer to militants from the liberal professions. Quite compelling, finally, was the similarity of the voting patterns of poor and wealthy residential districts during the oligarchic state period. Ecological data from the 1930s through the 1960s suggest that social class had little bearing on party or candidate choice: the poor displayed no greater tendency to support the worker-oriented APRA nor any lesser tendency to support conservatives such as General Manuel Odría than did voters in wealthy districts of the city.

In the contemporary period, too, the conceptions of poverty found in dominant ideology coincided with poor people's conceptions of themselves. One example was the enduring notion that poverty and inequality are inevitable and should be accepted with humility. Poor people themselves used the term *resentidos* to assail other poor people who protested their lot. Another idea shared by the dominant and the lowly was that poor communities can and should improve themselves by calling on their own resources and energies. This bootstrap theory of community development was long promoted by a conservative political leadership, epitomized by Pedro Beltrán in the 1950s, and is echoed today by shantytown leaders who would prefer to moderate the demands on the state voiced by their more unruly neighbors. As a statement of fact the bootstraps theory is half-true: poor communities like Independencia have probably made much greater contributions than wealthy communities in time, labor, and even (proportional to their incomes) money to develop services and infrastructure. But as an ethic of self-help the theory commands only limited support in today's shantytowns, where activists like Rosario Huayta respond, "The people don't have enough to eat, so how can you expect us to work Saturdays and Sundays also?" These answers to the first question suggest answers to the second.

2. *Do these elements of dominant discourse, mirrored in popular consciousness, promote the power of the dominant?* Here again the issue is partly whether that portion of lower-class mentality that has been penetrated by dominant culture, what Gramsci called "common sense," actually ends up perpetuating the power of the dominant and partly what the latter's purpose is in promoting it. All of the strands

of dominant discourse that we have identified as lodged in either earlier or contemporary popular mentalities enjoin the poor to accept social hierarchies as both unchangeable and proper. When the archbishop of Lima wrote that "poverty is the most certain path toward human happiness" that "only the State that triumphs in making the poor appreciate the spiritual treasures of poverty can resolve its social problems," he clearly saw the acceptance of poverty not only as the proper Christian attitude but also as a means of keeping social peace. And it is tempting to conclude that when public school manuals spoke of "categories established by nature, by society, and by God himself" and thus exhorted pupils to give "preferential treatment to some people over others," the schools were promoting a social ideology that was reinforced by the interests of dominant classes and institutions.

This is not to say that these efforts at intellectual domination always succeeded, even during the apex of the oligarchic state in Peru. After all, verbal and symbolic messages contain ambiguities, and a certain slippage may take place between the intentions of those producing them and the understanding of those receiving them. The bootstraps theory of community development is a good example of such ambiguities and shades of meaning. In Independencia the bootstraps theory was partially a rhetorical stratagem of conservative leaders who wished to attract the attention of housing ministry bureaucrats. But the theory also suggested a working-class effectiveness and self-reliance that ran counter to other strains in dominant ideology, such as the belief that poverty was a sign of weakness, stupidity, or laziness, inherent traits that would make even organized groups of poor people ineffective at achieving goals without the help of the better endowed. The Peruvian state's insistence on the self-reliance of poor communities over the years may ironically have helped lay the groundwork for a more assertive and demanding popular culture.

The mechanisms and settings that the dominant used to promote their discourse in Peru would have surprised Gramsci little. He saw formal theology and especially formal education as essential mechanisms for promulgating "common sense."[13] As a witness of fascism, Gramsci might not have been surprised, either, by the contradictory impact of APRA on popular consciousness during the oligarchic state period, exalting workers' rights and abilities at the same time that it called for deference to educated "professionals." He might, however, have been surprised to learn how the church and the schools and indeed the state itself were, with the decline of the oligarchic state, so central to the forging of a counterhegemony.

3. Is the apparent internalizing of dominant discourse and values by the lowly more than a pose? Far from being a strategic posture aimed at appealing to the vanity of the powerful, the pieces of lower-class political culture that reflected dominant discourse represented an authentic way of seeing the world. The clientelist did not shift to combative ideas and practices from one day to the next or from one campaign for services to another. Although these alternative world-views were not rigidly consistent, they were enduring mental templates that changed only when the settings and content of political socialization changed.

4. Does apparently consensual or accommodating outward behavior reflect the subordinate class actor's realistic assessment that any other kind of behavior would bring repression? There was plenty of repression—threatened and executed—on the streets of Lima's poor barrios. In Independencia in the 1980s and early 1990s the level of repression rose and fell largely as a function of events outside the district. States of emergency were imposed when members of the ruling party were attacked by guerrillas, after prison uprisings, or after the 1992 military coup. Emergencies meant that the Civil Guard officers housed in the local commissary could act more aggressively than usual to cut short neighborhood assemblies or meetings of "popular dining halls." Even when no state of emergency was in effect, armored cars filled with Civil Guard officers often drove along district roads, sometimes stopping pedestrians or drivers and demanding to see documents or inspect cars.

The Peruvian state was threatened, after all, by a serious insurrection, and the authorities interpreted civic activism as very close to subversion. Strikes, rallies to press for running water, open-air assemblies of neighborhood committees—in a context of enormous tensions and a defensive state, security forces were capable of seeing all of these as subversive and of treating those involved as suspects. Nevertheless, local "radicals" continued to act in ways that could easily be mistaken for subversion; obviously repression did not limit political action to traditional clientelist patterns.

5. *Where subaltern groups have shifted away from a mentality bearing the imprint of dominant values and beliefs, how do members of those groups understand that process?* To the extent that subalterns themselves offer interpretations of a shift from a hegemonic to a critical worldview, their interpretations will help neutralize arguments of skeptics like James Scott. These accounts work against the notion that apparent consent among subalterns is a strategic posture, a pose. Second, they negate the argument that those who see signs of "false consciousness" among subalterns just want to impose their own version of true consciousness for ulterior political reasons. One may understand the dynamics of cultural domination by taking seriously the views of the poor and powerless who themselves understand the workings of such influences in their own lives.

We saw evidence from Independencia that class- and rights-conscious residents were aware of a shift in their political-cultural orientation. The terms they used to describe this shift implied much more than a superficial adjustment of strategy or tactics. They spoke of a new understanding of themselves as effective agents of change. Rosario Huayta, who once believed that anything she said in public would be "stupid," came to see, through the encouragement of a party organizer and her experience fighting for community services, that she could be an effective public speaker. Julia Romero was recognizing a certain learned passivity in her relationship with the church when she recalled "showing respect" for priests, who were the highest authority in her highland community, and, later in Lima, "thinking all was well" when she merely attended mass. She criticized this earlier passivity later when she stated that "before there was no participation." A similar recognition of a change in one's own consciousness was voiced by Laura Sánchez, a Las Flores Mothers' Club member. Before joining the club, Sánchez thought that her poverty and problems were the result of her own idiosyncratic deficiencies. Later she learned that her problems "were not mine alone. . . . It's just that everyone is in his own place."

The concept of hegemony, then, lends considerable insight into the dynamics of both clientelism and new social movements in Peru. Still, there are perspectives on dominant-class ideological control that this account does not support. Marxist and critical theorists have tended toward various forms of a "dominant ideology thesis," which explains the survival of capitalism by positing the ability of the bourgeoisie (or institutions furthering its interests) to impose consent on workers through ideological manipulation. This thinking is much criticized, and appropriately so, for its excessive instrumentalism and lack of sensitivity to the slippage, inversions, and reinterpretations that ideologies (like other symbolic systems) can undergo.[14] It is unlikely, furthermore, that subaltern mentalities are ever the product of a single set of influences. Gramsci, as noted in chapter 1, posited at least two sources of consciousness of the "man-in-the-mass . . . one which is implicit in his activity and which in reality unites him with all his fellow-workers in the practical transformation of the real world; and one, superficially explicit or verbal, which he has inherited from the past and uncritically absorbed"; the result is "contradictory consciousness."[15] James Scott also implies two sources of poor peasants' consciousness: the social relations of paddy production and the "normative context" (in Scott's view something like a dominant ideology—the "public transcript"—exists, but the poor do not absorb it).[16]

In Peru too, even in the heyday of the oligarchic state and its attendant dominant ideology of fatalism and personal dependence, experiences that poor people regularly had and that contradicted dominant ideology must at the least have kept this ideology from fully shaping their consciousness. Facing a phalanx of armed mounted police set on throwing them off the land must surely have created chinks in any uncritical conception of the state as beneficent and paternal. Consequently, when a competing conception of the state— that of a class state that only through pressure tactics could be made to bend to the interests of poor people—presented itself, it found support among poor people.

But the story of counterhegemony told here cautions us to think broadly about the sources of alternative consciousness. There is no reason to privilege the workplace, or social relations tied to production, as the sole source of experiences that create chinks. Nor is there any reason to privilege political parties, Gramsci's "modern prince," as sources of counterhegemony. In Peru counterhegemonic ideas came, more or less simultaneously, from a range of sources: unions, schools, nuns, parties, state officials. And this happened not as a consequence of a change in the organization of production but, above all, because of the fairly accidental fact that some military officers began to think differently about the needs of their nation and then (briefly) gained state power.

Finally, when analysts argue that a social order rests on the intellectual domination of the lower classes, they often conceptualize a dichotomy between domination and autonomy. Gramsci contrasted "autonomous" conceptions of the world to the "submissive and subordinate" conceptions that subaltern classes adopt in "normal times."[17] Following a similar logic, Steven Lukes proposes observing "how people behave in 'abnormal times'—when the apparatus of power is removed or relaxed."[18] The method is similar to Scott's method of listening to the words of the weak when they speak outside of the range of the powerful. In considering the nature of hegemonic influence I also turned to an imagined "autonomous" worker's consciousness.

In Peru the power of the oligarchic state was relaxed, to say the least, when the "oligarchy" lost state power. And the answer to the question I asked in the first chapter—whether the powerful ever succeed in making the weak unaware of needs and interests that the weak would otherwise be conscious of—is yes. But *otherwise* in this case does not mean when subaltern culture is untouched by nonsubalterns. Counterhegemony was not lower-class consciousness fixed autonomously. Counterhegemonic belief systems (in this case that of "radicals") were themselves shaped by influences from outside the popular sectors. In Peru, institutions such as political parties, the church, and even the state itself, none of which could be described easily as controlled by the lower classes, were in the 1970s and thereafter sources of counterhegemonic conceptions of the world.

This fact can be acknowledged without going to the extreme of saying that political-cultural change in lower-class Peru amounted to nothing more than one dominant idea system's displacing another. First of all, this position would ignore the role of subaltern classes themselves in actively shaping the cultural world in which they live, through such processes as the independent creation of symbols and

discourse or the reinterpretation, inversion, or only partial assimilation of ideas coming from the outside. What is more important,
although it would be ludicrous to describe clientelism as a form of
false consciousness and radicalism as true consciousness, it is also
undeniable that dominant society imparted ideas among the urban
poor that were inconsistent with the latter's lived experience and
relied much more heavily than did counterhegemonic groups on such
distorting ideas. Chief among these was the notion that poor communities could develop by drawing on their own resources, without
making demands of the government or others, a notion that clientelist
leaders held despite the fact that it contradicted their everyday practices of seeking out aid from wherever it might be found. To offer
another example, the clientelist mentality drew strength from the
tendency of some poor people to identify psychologically with members of higher social classes. It was hard to sit in Carlos Velásquez's
hovel, high in the hills of Independencia, and hear him stress the
importance of living at low altitude and caring for one's "social prestige," without sensing this illusory social identification with "professionals" (Velásquez's term). In part, this was an unconscious strategy
for acquiring some dignity in a society that finds many ways to deny
dignity to the poor. Still, it is another example of the ways that
dominant culture drew strength from interpretations and identifica-
tions that were inconsistent with the lived experience of the lower-
class actor.

Postscript

What promise do the makers of Peru's new social movements hold for the future of democracy in that country? Let me first make clear the tarnished state of democracy in Peru since 1992. In April of that year, in response to parliamentary criticisms of his economic and counterinsurgency policies, president Alberto Fujimori, with the help of the armed forces, orchestrated a coup d'état, closing the congress and suspending the thirteen-year-old constitution. Official statements and actions in the first days after the coup showed that Fujimori and his associates planned an indefinite interruption of constitutional rule. Later, bending to international pressure, the government initiated a process that would end in the election of a Democratic Constituent Assembly and the writing of a new constitution. The constitution, created by a pro-Fujimori majority in the Constitutional Assembly, has a much more authoritarian flavor than the liberal document it supersedes. It was narrowly approved in a November 1993 plebiscite.

The response of the urban lower classes to these events has been full of ambiguities, and not only because of the inherited ambiguity of lower-class political culture. The rights-oriented and participatory popular subculture might have been expected to throw up obstacles to the new authoritarian turn of the state in the early 1990s. But even before the coup, the radical style of political action and the goals it was meant to lead to were becoming less tenable.

The near dissolution of the partisan Left exposed radicals to danger and undermined their sense that striving for social transformation was realistic. After the Velasco years, the Left and the new movements of the urban poor developed in symbiosis with one another: the Left benefited from the movements' spread, and the movements drew institutional support and protection from the Left. We saw this symbiosis at work in the mid-1980s in the relationship between Independencia's United Left municipal administration and local activists. In 1989 the national United Left coalition broke apart, and no individual socialist party or smaller coalitions of Left parties replaced it. After 1990, Alberto Fujimori's steady rhetorical assaults on political parties, along with his changes in electoral rules, further debilitated the Left and the party system in general. The disappearance of the Left meant that unruly poor actors were exposed both to state repression and to Sendero's violence. When people like Julia Romero imagined a society in which "we all eat or no one eats," many of them imagined this happening in part through the Left's continued dominance of local government and its eventual taking of national power through elections. When the vehicle fell apart, the dream seemed remote and utopian.

Sendero Luminoso's shift to an urban strategy in the early 1990s meant that local political leaders in neighborhoods like Independencia became popular Sendero targets, and the state appeared incapable of protecting them. Sendero saw radical-style leaders as standing between them and power in the shantytowns. María Elena Moyano, the president of a women's organization and lieutenant mayor of a large working-class district, assassinated by Sendero gunmen in February 1992, is a painful example. In 1993, therefore, I found many in Independencia interpreting Fujimori's coup as a step toward reestablishing authority at the center of a society in which the center itself showed signs of disappearing. And when in September 1992, five months after the coup, a special police unit captured Abimael Guzmán, the Sendero leader, and much of Sendero's central committee, the impression of revived authority deepened.

Clientelists tended to greet this return to authority enthusiastically. Radicals had mixed feelings. Because they believed that active and open participation from below were essential to meaningful political life, they were troubled by the Peruvian state's authoritarian turn. But well before the coup, the space for democratic participation (as the radicals defined it) had been contracting. In the 1980s, the radicals had conceived of the Peruvian state as a class state, with a built-in inclination to help people of means and to ignore or cast aside people like themselves. But democracy promised the ability to mold this class state into a citizen's state, one that saw to the needs of those at the bottom as well as those at the top. They certainly associated democracy with a state constituted through electoral mechanisms. But even then, they saw democracy as contingent on the untiring pressure that social movements from below could bring to bear.

In conversations with Independencia residents in the early 1990s, I perceived a new way of thinking about democracy, one that was simpler and more ominous. This version, entertained even by some of the district's more politicized residents, might be thought of as the "historical" view of democracy. It went something like this: democracy returned to Peru in 1980 and produced three presidents, hyperinflation, unemployment, Sendero Luminoso, cholera, blackouts, chaos, loss of national self-esteem, an internal war with twenty-five thousand dead. The list might go on to include, say, the death in a plane crash in 1987 of the members of Alianza Lima, a much-loved professional soccer team.[1] The prevalence of the grim historical definition of democracy may help explain some support, or at least the absence of outrage, for Fujimori's coup even among radicals.

This is not to say that they yearned for a revival of full military rule. By the early 1990s public opinion surveys showed that up to one-third of Lima's lower classes supported a return to military rule; but activists in the mold of Rosario Huayta were not necessarily among them.[2] Even though they remembered the Velasco regime fondly (as my survey showed), they knew that Peru's military was entirely changed since the fall of Velasco. Huayta and her counterparts, after all, spent a good deal of time trying to stay out of the way of the police and the military, whose presence in their daily lives took oppressive forms (the unmarked jeep filled with armed men driving through their neighborhoods, the water cannon standing poised to disperse the Feminine Committee when it demanded a health clinic).

The makers of Peru's new social movements felt that the world was closing in on them and that the suspending of parliamentary democracy could hardly make matters worse. The space that Velasco military rule opened up for them seemed, after a decade of civilian rule, to be disappearing under their feet. And as they perceived their unruly democratic practices as futile, and so exercised them less, so democracy itself became elusive.

Appendix

Identification number:

Name of supervisor:

Respondent's name:

Respondent's address:

Name of interviewer:

Interviewer's signature:

1. Age _____
2. Sex _____
3. Place of birth: Province _____
   District _____
4. (If not born in Lima) At what age did you arrive in Lima?

   _____

5. What year did you arrive in Independencia? _____
6. Did you live in another part of Lima before coming to
   Independencia? _____
   (Name of district)
7. How did you come to live here?
   a. Land invasion _____

    b. Bought land ____

    c. Rented home or room ____

    d. Other _____

8. Do you speak any language other than Spanish?

    _____

9. (For those who speak Quechua or Aymara) Which is your first language? _____

10. At what grade level did your studies end? ____

11. Do you know how to read and write? ____

12. Do you live in the high or low part of (name of sub-district)?
    High ____ Middle ____ Low ____

13. How many people live in your household? ____

14. What is your occupation? _____

15. What was your occupation before the present one?

    _____

16. What is your spouse's occupation? _____

17. Do you or have you ever belonged to a union?
    Yes ____ No ____
    And your spouse?
    Yes ____ No ____

18. Who else of the members of your household works?

    _____

19. What is the weekly income of your household?

    _____

20. What organizations exist in your neighborhood?

Organization	Participate?	Positions held?
a.		
b.		
c.		
d.		
e.		

21. How many meetings do you attend each week, including those of all of the organizations you belong to?

    a. 0 ____ b. 1 ____ c. 2–4 ____ d. 5 or more ____

22. Do the organizations you belong to receive support from any institution? ____ In what does this support consist?

    a. _____

    b. _____

    c. _____

23. What issues *(reclamos)* do you remember people in your neighborhood organizing around?

    Issue   Form of organizing   Year   Did you take part?

    a. _____

    b. _____

    c. _____

    d. _____

    e. _____

24. Do you sympathize with any political party? Which one?

    _____

25. Do (did) your parents sympathize with a political party, or tend to vote for a particular party?

    Father _____

    Mother _____

26. In what year did you vote for the first time? _____

    Whom did you vote for in the following elections?

27. *1978 Constituent Assembly*

    APRA (Haya de la Torre) ____ PSR (Rodríguez) ____

    PPC (Bedoya) ____ PCP (del Prado) ____

    FOCEP (Blanco) ____ UDP (Malpica) ____

28. *1980 Presidential*

    AP (Belaúnde) ____ PRT (Blanco) ____

    PPC (Bedoya) ____ UI (del Prado) ____

APRA (Villanueva) _____ UNIR (Breña) _____

UDP (Malpica) _____

29. *1980 Municipal*

Lima: Independencia:

AP (Orrego) _____   Slate #6 (Cáceres) _____

APRA (Debarbieri) _____   ARI (Atahualpa) _____

PPC (Amiel) _____   AP (Loja) _____

IU (Barrantes) _____   APRA (Quesada) _____

30. *1983 Municipal*

Lima: Independencia:

AP (Grados) _____   AP (Raza) _____

APRA (Barnechea) _____   APRA (Quesada) _____

IU (Barrantes) _____   IU (Moreno) _____

                                   PPC (Dolorier) _____

                                   PRT (Cocha) _____

31. *1985 Presidential*

AP (Alva Orlandini) _____ APRA (García) _____

PPC/CODE (Bedoya) _____ IU (Barrantes) _____

32. In this year's municipal elections, whom will you vote for?

Lima _____

Independencia _____

33. Who do you think will win? _____

34. (For those who always vote for the same party) Why do you vote for (name of party)? _____

35. (For those whose vote has varied) How do you decide for whom to vote? _____

36. What was your opinion of the Velasco military government?

_____

37. What was your opinion of the Morales Bermúdez military government? _____

38. What was your opinion of the recent Belaúnde government?

   _____

39. What is your opinion of the García government? _____

   _____

40. What is your opinion of the Barrantes municipal administration?

   _____

41. What is your opinion of the Moreno district municipal administration? _____

42. Do you think, in general, that one obtains better results through struggle methods *(medidas de lucha)* or legal petitioning *(trámites legales)?* _____

43. Do you think the organizations in your neighborhood should depend on the central government? Yes ____ No ____

44. Do you think it important that organizations in your neighborhood work with organizations in other neighborhoods?
   Yes ____ No ____

45. Do you think organizations in your neighborhood should work with political parties?
   Yes ____ No ____

46. Imagine that you (or your spouse) is out of work, and you are offered a job in a factory. As a condition for accepting the job, you must promise not to join the union in the factory. What would you do? _____

   _____

Notes

Chapter 1

1. Rosario Huayta is a pseudonym. I use pseudonyms throughout to refer to Independencia residents except the district's mayor, who is a well-known public official. I also use pseudonyms for names of individual barrios or neighborhoods within the district; however, Independencia and the names of other major subsections within the district, such as Tawantinsuyu and Ermitaño, are real names.

2. See, respectively, James C. Scott, *Weapons of the Weak: Everyday Forms of Peasant Resistance* (New Haven: Yale University Press, 1985); John Gaventa, *Power and Powerlessness: Quiescence and Rebellion in an Appalachian Valley* (Urbana: University of Illinois Press, 1980); Youseff Cohen, *The Manipulation of Consent: The State and Working-Class Consciousness in Brazil* (Pittsburgh: University of Pittsburgh Press, 1989); and Mathew A. Crenson, *The Un-Politics of Air Pollution: A Study of Non-Decisionmaking in the Cities* (Baltimore: Johns Hopkins University Press, 1971).

3. Theda Skocpol, *States and Social Revolutions: A Comparative Analysis of France, Russia, and China* (Cambridge: Cambridge University Press, 1979).

4. Ibid., 14–15.

5. See Michael Taylor, "Rationality and Revolutionary Collective Action," in Taylor, ed., *Rationality and Revolution* (Cambridge: Cambridge University Press, 1988); Samuel Popkin, "Political Entrepreneurs and Peasant Movements in Vietnam," ibid.; and Dennis Chong, *Collective Action and the Civil Rights Movement* (Princeton: Princeton University Press, 1991).

6. Scott, *Weapons of the Weak;* idem, *Domination and the Arts of Resistance: Hidden Transcripts* (New Haven: Yale University Press, 1990).

7. Karl Marx and Friedrich Engels, *The German Ideology,* ed. and trans. R. Pascal (New York: International Publishers, 1947), 39.

8. Here I use Joseph Femia's translation of Gramsci's *Il materialismo storico e la filosofia di Benedetto Croce* from "Hegemony and Consciousness in the Thought of Antonio Gramsci," *Political Studies* 23, no. 1 (1975): 33. Femia's translation of these passages is more faithful to the Italian in several respects than is that of Quintin Hoare and Geoffrey Nowell Smith in *Selections from the Prison Notebooks* (New York: International Publishers, 1971). Unless otherwise noted, however, I have relied on the translations of Hoare and Nowell Smith.

9. Gramsci, "Il materialismo storico," as cited in Femia, "Hegemony and Consciousness," 33.

10. Ibid.

11. Controversy swirls around the meaning of the term *hegemony* as understood by Gramsci. See Perry Anderson, "The Antinomies of Antonio Gramsci," *New Left Review* 100 (1977): 5–78; and Adam Przeworski, *Capitalism and Social Democracy* (Cambridge: Cambridge University Press, 1985), chapter 4.

12. Recent studies of social movements, in Latin America and elsewhere, that are consistent with this approach include Cohen, *Manipulation of Consent;* Gaventa, *Power and Powerlessness;* Sonia Alvarez, *Engendering Democracy in Brazil: Women's Movements in Transition Politics* (Princeton: Princeton University Press, 1990); Doug McAdam, *Political Process and the Development of Black Insurgency, 1930–1979* (Chicago: University of Chicago Press, 1982); E. P. Thompson, "The Moral Economy of the English Crowd in the Eighteenth Century," *Past and Present,* no. 50 (1971): 7–136; Ron Eyerman and Andrew Jamison, *Social Movements: A Cognitive Approach* (University Park: Pennsylvania State University Press, 1991); and Alberto Melucci, *Nomads of the Present* (Philadelphia, Pa.: Temple University Press, 1989).

Other recent studies of Latin American social movements include Scott Mainwaring, *The Catholic Church and Politics in Brazil, 1916–1985* (Stanford: Stanford University Press, 1986); Elizabeth Jelin, ed., *Movimientos sociales y democracia emergente,* 2 vols. (Buenos Aires: Centro Editor de América Latina, 1987); idem, *Los nuevos movimientos sociales,* 2 vols. (Buenos Aires: Centro Editor de América Latina, 1985); Fernando Calderón G., ed., *Los movimientos sociales ante la crisis* (Buenos Aires: CLACSO, 1986); David Slater, ed., *New Social Movements and the State in Latin America* (Amsterdam: CEDLA, 1985); Arturo Escobar and Sonia Alvarez, eds., *The Making of Social Movements in Latin America* (Boulder, Colo.: Westview, 1992); Susan Eckstein, "Power and Popular Protest," in Eckstein, ed., *Power and Popular Protest: Latin American Social Movements* (Berkeley and Los Angeles: University of California Press, 1989), 1–66; and Alain Touraine, *Actores sociales y sistemas políticos en América Latina* (Santiago: PREALC/ OIT, 1987).

13. Scott, *Weapons of the Weak,* 309. "Public legitimacy" should not be read as connoting legitimacy from the point of view of the subaltern actor, since Scott believes that subalterns never find legitimate the institutions and practices that apparently justify social domination.

14. But if efforts at protest and rebellion have met with defeat or if the practical political situation is heavily stacked against protest and rebellion, then a resigned belief in the impracticality of change ought not to be considered evidence of the domination and control of subaltern consciousness.

15. The Christian beliefs that "the meek shall inherit the earth" and "the last shall be first" are examples of this principle: poverty and powerlessness are rewarded in the afterlife.

16. See Alfred Stepan, *The State and Society: Peru in Comparative Perspective* (Princeton: Princeton University Press, 1978).

17. See, e.g., Joshua Cohen and Joel Rogers, "Secondary Associations and Democratic Governance," *Politics and Society* 20, no. 4 (1992): 393–472.

18. Lima has two levels of government, one elected by voters in the greater municipal area (the "provincial" administration), the other elected in each of forty-one districts.

19. I also considered ways in which this peculiarity of the district might make it less useful as a field site. For example, did the relative success of local women in achieving positions of political leadership mean that Independencia's female population was unusually assertive, mobilized, or politicized? In fact, in other districts I found similar examples of female leaders in charge of various local institutions, even though none had reached the position of mayor.

20. I decided not to live in Independencia for the following reasons. When I first went to Lima in 1985 to begin this research project, and before I had selected Independencia as a field site, I moved in with a family in La Victoria, an older working-class district. A few months after I arrived, several people accused of running a Sendero Luminoso safe house a few blocks away were arrested, and much was made of the fact that some of the accused were "white" and "foreign" (one of the accused, Sibila Arredondo, was the fair-skinned, Chilean widow of the noted writer and anthropologist José María Arguedas). Both my host family and I were very concerned that my presence in their household might bring suspicion upon them. The episode and our decision that I should leave their home was a sad reflection of the deteri-

orating political situation in Peru in the mid-1980s. Under more favorable circumstances living in Independencia would have contributed significantly to my fieldwork there.

Chapter 2

1. The term *oligarchic state* is used to describe a prepopulist period in many Latin American countries, when agricultural exporters were in control of the state or at least defined economic policy. The relative weakness of the populist challenge meant that the oligarchic state period was prolonged in Peru.

2. See Carl H. Landé, "The Dyadic Basis of Clientelism," in *Friends, Followers, and Factions: A Reader in Political Clientelism,* ed. Steffan W. Schmidt et al. (Berkeley and Los Angeles: University of California Press, 1977); and S. N. Eisenstadt and L. Roniger, "Patron-Client Relations as a Model of Structuring Social Exchange," *Comparative Studies in Society and History* 22, no. 1 (1980): 42–77. For studies that place clientelism in a more macrohistorical Latin American context, see Nicos Mouzelis, "On the Concept of Populism: Populist and Clientelist Modes of Incorporation in Semiperipheral Polities," *Politics and Society* 14, no. 3 (1985): 332; Philippe C. Schmitter, "Paths to Political Development in Latin America," in *Changing Latin America,* ed. Douglas A. Chalmers (New York: Academy of Political Science, Columbia University, 1972), 83–109; and Robert R. Kaufman, "Corporatism, Clientelism, and Partisan Conflict: A Study of Seven Latin American Countries," in *Authoritarianism and Corporatism in Latin America,* ed. James M. Malloy (Pittsburgh: University of Pittsburgh Press, 1977).

3. The concept of upper-class affinity parallels Charles R. Hales's concept of "Anglo affinity" (see *Resistance and Contradiction: Miskitu Indians and the Nicaraguan State, 1894–1987* [Stanford: Stanford University Press, 1994], 83). Whereas Hale stresses admiration for dominant ideas and values, I add a sense of identification: a subset of the poor sees itself as being not fundamentally different from members of higher social classes.

4. Some examples are offered later in this chapter, and others can be found in Henry A. Dietz, "Bureaucratic Demand-Making and Clientelistic Participation in Peru," in Malloy, *Authoritarianism and Corporatism in Latin America;* idem, *Poverty and Problem-Solving under Military Rule* (Austin: University of Texas Press, 1980); and David Collier, *Squatters and Oligarchs: Authoritarian Rule and Policy Change in Peru* (Baltimore: Johns Hopkins University Press, 1976).

5. On the early history of APRA, see Peter Klarén, *Modernization, Dislocation, and Aprismo: Origins of the Peruvian Aprista Party, 1870–1932* (Austin: University of Texas Press, 1973); Steve Stein, *Populism in Peru: The Emergence of the Masses and the Politics of Social Control* (Madison: University of Wisconsin Press, 1980); and Carmen Rosa Balbi, *El Partido Comunista y el APRA en la crisis de los años treinta* (Lima: G. Herrera, 1980). A definitive history of the Peruvian Communist Party has yet to be written. Alberto Flores Galindo's "Prólogo" to *El pensamiento comunista* (Lima: Mosca Azul, 1982) provides the outlines of this history.

6. I am not claiming that Peruvian society as a whole was free of class conflict or labor militancy during the oligarchic state period. My claim is much narrower: that in the middle decades of the twentieth century, and among organizations growing out of urban residential communities in the capital city, a series of factors conspired to lower the level of open conflict and to press collective action among the poor into clientelist channels.

7. The connection between features of the Peruvian state and political system outlined here and the country's economic history (export orientation and relatively late import-substitution industrialization in comparison with those in other South American countries) is laid out in Rosemary Thorp and Geoffrey Bertram, *Peru, 1890–1977: Growth and Policy in an Open Economy* (London: Macmillan, 1978).

8. Stein, *Populism in Peru*, 27off.

9. Gonzálo Portocarrero and Patricia Oliart, *El Perú desde la escuela* (Lima: Instituto de Apoyo Agrario, 1989).

10. Francisco García Calderón, *En torno al Perú y América* (Lima: Juan Mejía Baca y P. C. Villanueva, 1954), cited in Steve Stein, "Populism and Mass Politics in Peru: The Political Behavior of the Working Classes in the 1931 Presidential Election" (Ph.D. diss., Stanford University, 1973), 520.

11. Manuel Antonio Carreño, *Manual de urbanidad y buenas maneras* (Lima: Ediciones "El Perú y sus leyes," 1966), 39, cited in Stein, "Populism and Mass Politics in Peru," 529.

12. Cited in Julio Cotler, *Clases, estado, y nación en el Perú* (Lima: Instituto de Estudios Peruanos, 1978), 308. Unless indicated otherwise, all translations from the Spanish are my own.

13. Antonio Gramsci, *Selections from the Prison Notebooks*, ed. and trans. Quintin Hoare and Geoffrey Nowell Smith (New York: International Publishers, 1971), 331.

14. In addition to Stein's *Populism in Peru*, see his "El vals criollo y los valores de la clase trabajadora en la Lima de comienzos del siglo XX," *Socialismo y Participación*, no. 17 (March 1982), 43–50.

15. Stein, "El vals criollo," 49.

16. Quoted in ibid., 48. The one waltz Stein found that contained themes contrary to the predominant fatalism and deference was called "The Plebeian" ("El Plebeyo"). In this song the protagonist, who has been spurned by an aristocratic woman, declares: "My blood, although plebeian / is just as red / Señor, why aren't beings / All of the same value?"

17. Arturo Sabroso, interview by Steve Stein, January 29, 1971, cited in Stein, *Populism in Peru*, 155.

18. Stein, *Populism in Peru*, 195ff. See also Rafael Roncagliolo, *Quién ganó? Elecciones, 1931–1980* (Lima: DESCO, 1980); and Jorge Basadre, *Elecciones y centralismo en el Péru* (Lima: Centro de Investigación de la Universidad del Pacífico, 1980).

19. Sandra Powell, "Political Participation in the Barriadas: A Case Study," *Comparative Political Studies* 2, no. 2 (1969): 195–215.

20. Henry A. Dietz, "Political Participation in the Barriadas: An Extension and Reexamination," *Comparative Political Studies* 18, no. 3 (1985): 323–55.

21. See ibid., 335 (table 4).

22. See José Matos Mar, *Las barriadas de Lima, 1957* (Lima: Instituto de Estudios Peruanos, 1967).

23. Earlier research in Peru has shown, however, that the shantytowns are not the rural migrant's first point of contact with the city. Anthony Leeds and Elizabeth Leeds, among others, show that in both Lima and Rio de Janeiro most rural migrants lived first in older inner-city neighborhoods before moving to the shantytowns (see "Brazil and the Myth of Urban Rurality: Urban Experience, Work, and Values in 'Squatments' of Rio de Janeiro and Lima," in *City and Country in the Third World: Issues in the Modernization of Latin America*, ed. Arthur J. Field [Cambridge: Schenkman, 1970], 229–72, 277–85). My research in Independencia confirmed this finding. One-quarter of a sample of 985 district residents of voting age were, in 1986, young people who were born in Independencia. Of the remaining respondents, a full 95 percent had moved there from other, older sections of Lima. For more details on the survey see chapter 6.

24. David Collier reports that as of the end of the 1960s, 44 percent of squatted land was publicly owned, 19 percent was privately owned, and 35 percent was the subject of ownership disputes (*Squatters and Oligarchs*, 35).

25. David Collier reports a case in the late fifties when an APRA-affiliated union claimed ownership of lands that invaders were occupying east of Lima in order to help justify the squatters' eviction (see ibid., chap. 5).

26. See Dietz, *Poverty and Problem-Solving under Military Rule;* Wayne Cornelius, *Politics and the Migrant Poor in Mexico City* (Stanford: Stanford

University Press, 1975); Janet Perlman, *The Myth of Marginality: Urban Politics in Rio de Janeiro* (Berkeley: Campus Books, 1976); and L. Lomnitz, *Networks and Marginality: Life in a Mexican Shantytown* (New York: Academic, 1977).

27. Susan Lobo, *A House of My Own: Social Organization in the Squatter Settlements of Lima, Peru* (Tucson: University of Tucson Press, 1982), 65.

28. Cited in Etienne Henry, *La escena urbana: Estado y movimientos de pobladores, 1968–1976* (Lima: Pontificia Universidad Católica del Perú, 1978), 37.

29. What follows is reconstructed from oral accounts, unpublished documents, and newspaper stories.

30. *El Comercio,* November 18, 1960.

31. Ibid.

32. Ibid., November 25, 1960.

33. The squatters rejected this proposal "because there are strange animals in the jungle and because they are accustomed to the city" (ibid.).

Chapter 3

1. This unusual experience of military rule provoked enormous interest among scholars. For a review of major works see Martin J. Scurrah, "Military Reformism in Peru: Opening the Pandora's Box," *Latin American Research Review* 21, no. 1 (1986): 244–57.

2. The most detailed description of these internal differences is to be found in Henry Pease García, *El ocaso del poder oligárquico: Lucha política en la escena oficial, 1968–75* (Lima: DESCO, 1977); and idem, *Los caminos al poder: Tres años de crisis en la escena política* (Lima: DESCO, 1979).

3. For a conceptual comparison of corporatism, pluralism, and other systems of interest representation, see Philippe C. Schmitter, "Still the Century of Corporatism?" in *The New Corporatism: Social-Political Structures in the Iberian World,* ed. Frederick B. Pike and Thomas Stritch (Notre Dame: University of Notre Dame Press, 1974), 93. For important applications of the concept of corporatism in Latin America, see Guillermo O'Donnell, "Corporatism and the Question of the State," in *Authoritarianism and Corporatism in Latin America,* ed. James M. Malloy (Pittsburgh: University of Pittsburgh Press, 1977); David Collier and Ruth Berins Collier, "Inducements versus Constraints: Disaggregating 'Corporatism,'" *American Political Science Review* 73, no. 4 (1979): 967–86; and Alfred Stepan, *The State and Society: Peru in Comparative Perspective* (Princeton: Princeton University Press, 1978). Many authors use the term "corporatist" in association with the Velasco regime, but Stepan has developed this theme the furthest.

4. Evelyne Huber Stephens notes that this increase in Peru was proportionally greater than that in Chile in the years 1966–72, despite the high rate of unionizing in the latter country during the Frei and Allende periods ("The Peruvian Military Government, Labor Mobilization, and the Political Strength of the Left," *Latin American Research Review* 18, no. 2 [1983]: 67–68).

5. Carmen Rosa Balbi, *Identidad clasista en el sindicalismo* (Lima: DESCO, 1989).

6. See Stephens, "The Peruvian Military Government."

7. The same is not strictly true of the peasantry, since in 1961–63 a Trotskyite party under Hugo Blanco provided the leadership for a peasant movement in the Cuzco region. I am claiming not that the Velasco regime literally created the partisan Left in the 1970s but that the regime produced opportunities that a nascent and relatively isolated Left took advantage of, thus transforming itself into a major political force during the period following military rule (see chapter 4). The Soviet-line Communist Party had roots in Mariátegui's Socialist Party, founded in the 1920s (see chapter 2). Several Trotskyite parties had existed since the 1940s, and in the early 1960s the Soviet-Chinese split created a schism within Peru's Communist Party that created Maoist parties, later to become very important. Peru also experienced some unsuccessful, *foco*-style guerrilla movements in the early and mid-1960s, as well as the much more successful peasant movement of Hugo Blanco. In connection with the germination of the Left in the 1960s, prior to the Velasco coup, should be mentioned nationalist and developmentalist but less fully Marxist parties such as the Progressive Social Movement and intellectuals tied to journals such as *Sociedad y Política* (Aníbal Quijano), as well as intellectuals in institutions such as the Instituto de Estudios Peruanos (Salazar Bondy, José Matos Mar, and others). Equally important were the left wings of APRA and AP: both parties experienced schisms in the 1960s, with defectors founding socialist parties (the Movement of the Revolutionary Left [MIR] and the Revolutionary Vanguard [VR], respectively). All of this ferment preceded the Velasco regime, and the regime's own left wing itself was tied to various of the parties, intellectual movements, and even guerrilla activities mentioned here. See Ricardo Letts, *La izquierda peruana: Organizaciones y tendencias* (Lima: Mosca Azul, 1981); and Eugenio Chang-Rodríguez, *Opciones políticas peruanas* (Lima: Centro de Documentación Andina, 1985), chaps. 7, 8, and 10.

8. Dietz reports correlations between the percentages of blue-collar and of squatter populations in Lima's residential districts of .54 in the 1961 census and .83 in the 1981 census (Henry A. Dietz, "Political Participation in the Barriadas: An Extension and Reexamination," *Comparative Political Studies*

18, no. 3 [1985]: 331). It is probable that many blue-collar workers living in poor districts were themselves squatters.

9. I draw here from various works, including Dietz, *Poverty and Problem-Solving under Military Rule* (Austin: University of Texas Press, 1980); David Collier, *Squatters and Oligarchs: Authoritarian Rule and Policy Change in Peru* (Baltimore: Johns Hopkins University Press, 1976); Stepan, *State and Society;* Etienne Henry, *La escena urbana: Estado y movimientos de pobladores, 1968–1976* (Lima: Pontificia Universidad Católica del Perú, 1978); and Gustavo Riofrío and Alfredo Rodríguez, *De invasores a invadidos*, 2d ed. (Lima: DESCO, 1980).

10. Stepan forcefully makes this point in comparing the military government's ability to make headway with squatters with its much more limited success among coastal sugar workers, where APRA had been very active for many years (see his *State and Society,* chaps. 5 and 6).

11. On the structure and role of SINAMOS, see ibid.; and Carlos Franco, *Perú: Participación popular* (Lima: Centro de Estudios sobre el Desarrollo y la Participación, 1979).

12. Dietz, "Bureaucratic Demand-Making and Clientelistic Participation in Peru," in Malloy, *Authoritarianism and Corporatism in Latin America,* 414.

13. Carlos Delgado, cited in ibid., 433.

14. Ibid., 421.

15. See, e.g., Teresa Tovar, *Velasquismo y movimiento popular: Historia del movimiento popular, 1968–1975* (Lima: DESCo, 1986).

16. Gonzálo Portocarrero and Patricia Oliart, *El Perú desde la escuela* (Lima: Instituto de Apoyo Agrario, 1986).

17. As Etienne Henry has shown, this problem plagued the housing ministry, where conservative Navy officials held control. Government expenditure was concentrated in relatively wealthy housing developments between 1970 and 1974. Henry calculates that public expenditures over this period in lower-class districts such as Independencia, Rímac, and Villa María del Triunfo amounted to 8 percent of expenditures in wealthy districts such as La Molina. Thus the housing ministry and SINAMOS were working at cross-purposes (see Henry, *La escena urbana*).

18. On the Velasco regime's shrinking resource base, see David Scott Palmer, *Peru: The Authoritarian Tradition* (New York: Praeger, 1980).

19. In the case of Maoist, Trotskyite, socialist Christian, Guevarist, and other leftist parties, the military regime did not just coincide with their emergence but actually helped, through various actions, to spawn or strengthen them. The causal links are complex and include the regime's peculiar mix of mobilizational rhetoric and actions with its relatively mild

repression. Unlike APRA, which was paralyzed by the military's "revolution," the new leftist forces took advantage of the opportunities opened up by the military and for the most part dodged its rather undeveloped repressive apparatus. One such new opportunity space was in labor organizing: most of the new parties of the Left joined in a tense alliance with the Communist Party and the CGTP and, as mentioned earlier, were extremely active in organizing new unions or wooing existing ones away from an *aprista* leadership. Of course many other international factors were involved in the rise of new Marxist parties in Peru, as elsewhere in Latin America, in the 1970s.

The strengthening of a socially oriented wing of the Catholic Church in contemporary Peru predated the Velasco regime; one would have to go back at least to the early 1960s and the founding, by Gustavo Gutiérrez and others, of the Oficina Nacional de Investigación Social (ONIS), an association of progressive clerics. But like the Left, the progressive church in Peru experienced a surge in membership and activities during the Velasco years; again a mix of domestic and international factors was at work.

20. This is not to say that these other actors were incapable of perpetuating their own brands of clientelism; that their impact in the shantytowns was also subtle and sometimes contradictory will be illustrated with examples from Independencia.

21. The survey, conducted in May and June 1986, coincided with the early, relatively successful phase of the García government. Predictably, conversations with Independencia residents on return visits in 1988 and 1989 revealed a drastic deterioration of the García image. I believe that the Velasco regime's approval rating in 1986 was higher than it would have been a decade earlier; the poor performance of subsequent governments probably was responsible for the gilded memory of Velasco among a majority of Independencia residents.

22. CIPEP and Municipalidad de Lima, *Plan de emergencia distrital* (Lima: n.d., mimeographed).

23. See Stepan, *State and Society;* and Collier and Collier, "Inducements versus Constraints."

24. The SINAMOS organizer in Independencia worked for the most "revolutionary" agency in a state that wished to effect a "revolution in participation." I can only speculate that he was unhappy with the neighborhood committee's obsequious dependence, perhaps just as unhappy as he was with the bothersome activism of the mothers' club.

25. This was especially true early in the regime, in such programs as health promotion and literacy drives. A nun and lay Catholic worker whom I interviewed also came first to the district as health promoters under a Velasco program.

26. The exceptions were the Soviet-line Communist Party, which, as outlined earlier, was allied with the Velasco government, and several Trotskyite parties (see Letts, *La izquierda peruana*).

27. Stepan and others discuss the close initial relationship between church leaders and Velasco: the regime's initial scheme for the shantytowns came from Bishop Bambarén, a bishop active in Lima's shantytowns, whom General Velasco consulted directly (see Stepan, *State and Society*, 161–62).

28. See Aldo Panfichi, "La crisis y las multitudes: Lima, 5 de febrero de 1975," *Debates en Sociología*, no. 9 (1983): 31–63.

29. "In Greece, Peru, and Argentina circa 1970," Guillermo O'Donnell and Philippe C. Schmitter remark, "the 'decision to open' was heavily influenced by the presence of strong opposition forces in the civilian population" (*Transitions from Authoritarian Rule: Tentative Conclusions about Uncertain Democracies* [Baltimore: Johns Hopkins University Press, 1986], 19–20). These authors later note the unusual strength of the "popular upsurge" in Peru as in Portugal and Venezuela.

30. See Oswaldo Reynoso, Vilma Aguilar, and Hildebrando Pérez H., *Luchas del magisterio: De Mariátegui al SUTEP* (Lima: Ediciones Narración, 1979).

31. One can speculate about the factors that produced an affinity between Peru's teachers and a radical politics (a pattern that is certainly not unknown in other national settings). Schoolteachers in Peru themselves come disproportionately from working-class backgrounds. In the late 1960s, when the number of working-class students first began to grow, the number of university students electing teacher training as their major field of study expanded by a factor of five. In contrast, the number of university students majoring in the humanities tripled, and those studying natural sciences and engineering doubled (see Enrique Bernales, *Movimientos sociales y movimientos universitarios en el Perú* [Lima: Pontificia Universidad Católica, 1975]). There is a wide disparity, furthermore, between the relatively high educational level of primary and secondary school teachers and their income. According to official statistics, in mid-1980 the average teacher's salary could purchase only 40 percent of a family food basket; during the first quarter of 1989 that figure had declined to 10 percent. Figures are from the Instituto Peruano de Planificación, reported in Hernando Burgos, "Maestros: La última clase," *QuéHacer*, no. 58 (April 1989): 32–49.

32. See Barbara Stallings, "Peru and the U.S. Banks: Privatization of Financial Relations," in *Capitalism and the State in U.S.–Latin American Relations*, ed. Richard R. Fagen (Stanford: Stanford University Press, 1979).

Chapter 4

1. See Henry A. Dietz, "Political Participation in the Barriadas: An Extension and Reexamination," *Comparative Political Studies* 18, no. 3 (1985).

2. Caution is required because the data on socioeconomic status are aggregated at the district level, whereas the voting data deal with individuals. See ibid., 331 ff., for a description of how district socioeconomic clusters were calculated. In the two other national elections in the years following military rule—the 1978 Constituent Assembly election and the 1980 presidential election—class-based voting patterns were also apparent.

3. See David Scott Palmer, ed., *The Shining Path of Peru* (New York: St. Martin's, 1992); and Orin Starn, "New Literature on Peru's Sendero Luminoso," *Latin American Research Review* 27, no. 2 (1992): 212–26.

4. To a lesser extent the Tupac Amaru Revolutionary Movement (Movimiento Revolucionario Tupac Amaru, or MRTA) also attracted this sort of following. The MRTA is a guerrilla organization descended from various Left parties of the 1970s that appeared in 1985; it has never commanded the strength of Sendero.

5. Concejo Distrital de Independencia, *Boletín Municipal,* January 1986. This reading is one of greater continuity between "movements" of squatters in the early 1960s and the municipal government than that laid out in chapter 2. There I argued that the early land drives fell short of being movements and that a deep ideological transformation giving a new flavor to lower-class politics, a flavor that Independencia's municipal administration aptly represented, occurred only under military rule in the 1970s. In informal conversations I had many opportunities to discuss this (and other topics of political analysis) with municipal staff members, who tended to agree that this "official" history glossed over qualitative differences between the land invasions and the movements initiated during the Velasco and Morales years.

6. The mayors of all parties rejected this proposal.

7. Mario Vargas Llosa's Movimiento Libertad, a third conservative political organization, appeared in 1987; it was greatly debilitated after Vargas Llosa's unsuccessful election campaign in 1990.

8. In the 1980s, Peru's Episcopal Council was sharply divided between bishops associated with liberation theology or at least espousing a social vision of the role of the church, on the one hand, and bishops who were more conservative and preferred that the church play a more purely spiritual role. Within Catholic circles this tension was expressed in terms of the "social" versus the "pastoral" role of the church.

9. None of the members of the communal dining halls had experience operating these large machines, so the job of sewing pants was contracted out

to the tailor husband of a member, who was eventually to be paid with proceeds from the sale of the pants. But the tailor, dubious of this arrangement, kept about 10 percent of the finished products as pay. Dining hall members were unable to reclaim these pants even after turning to the police. Communal dining hall members faced predictable problems in selling the pants that were returned, such as a lack of knowledge of markets and extremely low prices in the informal sector channels they eventually used to sell the clothing. Much of the clothing was eventually purchased by kitchen members themselves, thus transferring income from their households to the dining halls. All who were involved recognized in the end that the scheme had been a failure.

Chapter 5

1. Those who object to the simplification of this bifurcated account generally propose an alternative that is even more simplified: they prefer descriptions of lower-class political culture as unitary (rather than dichotomized) or, perhaps better, as absent. This view holds that lower-class actors have access to a single repertoire of tools that they strategically deploy according to the requirements of the moment; these actors are not characterized by any particular pattern of consciousness, and they approach the strategic tools available to them, and other actors whom they encounter, without any feelings, normative beliefs, values, habitual predispositions, and so forth. I would not rule out such a situation as impossible, but it does not reflect the nature of political culture in contemporary urban Peru. The mix of strategy and culture as determinants of action is discussed further in chapter 7.

Clientelism and radicalism did not exhaust the mentalities and behaviors of local political actors. Both of these patterns involved, for example, basically activist attitudes, although the two styles of activism are vastly different. Some of the people I encountered in Independencia were apathetic and disengaged from community affairs. Others showed signs of finding refuge in an otherworldly religiosity. This chapter will say less about them.

2. One activist who at the time of the research was a member of Independencia's district council was interviewed in his office. All of the interviews were voluntary and unpaid. I hope that the greatest hardship imposed by the interviews was that endured by Leoncio Mamani, who missed the televised final match of the 1986 soccer World Cup.

3. See chapter 6.

4. Other residents reported that there had been a SINAMOS presence. Mayta's lack of exposure to SINAMOS and other outside actors during the period of military rule helps explain her relative passivity later.

Chapter 6

1. Respondents were asked whether organizations in their neighborhood should, in the wording of the survey, "depend on" *(depender de)* the central government. To "depend on" in this context is widely understood as receiving financial support from an institution. Even for radicals the phrase "depend on" is not in itself pejorative: a wide range of organizations in the district described themselves as depending on the church, private, politically oriented centers, European nongovernmental organizations, and so forth.

2. Two of the attitudinal questions yielded ambiguous results, but for different reasons, I believe. Responses to the question "Should organizations in your neighborhood work with similar organizations in other neighborhoods?" originally intended to serve as a second measure of horizontal solidarity, elicited an overwhelmingly positive response: only 17 percent responded negatively, and responses displayed no patterned association with other attitudinal variables. I suspect that respondents found it too difficult to say no to this question, which therefore failed to measure the theorized underlying concept. The question involving the hypothetical job offer posed a more appealing set of alternatives and was a better measure of horizontal solidarity.

A similar anomaly appeared in response to a question about political parties. Qualitative interviews and observations had suggested a difference in the kind of relationship clients and radicals pursued with political parties: radicals were more party-oriented, whereas clients sought alliances with individual political or bureaucratic actors (see chapter 5). Survey respondents were asked whether they believed local organizations should work with political parties. Responses to this question were not what the radical/client model would lead one to predict. There was a slight tendency for those who opposed collaboration with political parties to accept the hypothetical job offer at a higher rate than did those who favored parties (as the radical/client model would predict), but the effect was slight (and significant only at the level of $p = .08$). On the other hand, there was a strong tendency of those wary of political parties to also oppose collaboration with the central government, a trend opposite to the radical/client model's predictions.

An explanation for this anomaly is that there may be a significant gap between the radicals' ideology and their practice in their relations with political parties. Radical leaders whom I interviewed at length often stated forcefully that political parties had no place in the internal operation of local organizations and that such organizations had to preserve "autonomy" from partisan politics. Indeed, the autonomy principle was so frequently voiced that during the early stages of my field research, as I first became aware of the sharp conflicts among local residents, I sensed that one of the recent innovations of local political life was the new-style political leaders' freeing local organizations from outside partisan influence. Only later, after much observation of the actual, day-to-day interactions between local leaders and political parties, did I become aware that the relationship was in fact the reverse: the radicalized leadership indeed enjoyed closer and more ideologically motivated ties with parties, whereas the clients, who were not averse to approaching parties for practical reasons, were more free-floating in partisan terms. The survey question may have accurately tapped the radicals' abstract belief in the autonomy of local organizations, but it masked the difference in practice between radicals and clients.

3. Principal component analysis revealed one factor with an eigenvalue greater than unity, with which all three attitudinal variables were positively correlated. In using eigenvalues of greater than one as a stopping criterion in factor analysis, I am following R. J. Rummel, *Applied Factor Analysis* (Evanston, Ill.: Northwestern University Press, 1970).

Principal Component Analysis of Attitudinal Variables

	1	2	3
Eigenvalue	1.274	0.926	0.710
Difference	0.348	0.126	
Proportion	0.425	0.309	0.267
Cumulative	0.425	0.733	1.000

Eigenvalues of the correlation matrix: total = 3, average = 1

4. Occupational differences were associated with the probability of exposure to labor unions, respondents involved in factory work being more likely than others to have some experience with labor unions. In this sense there is an indirect tie between occupational differentiation and political mentality, but the impact was mediated through union exposure.

5. A more finely tuned operationalization of the historical shift laid out earlier in this study would have distinguished not just between exposure and nonexposure to unions but between exposure to "classist" unions and both exposure to more conservative unions and nonexposure. In pretesting the survey instrument, however, it became clear that there was no easy way to get at this difference.

6. With regard to this last point, one might speculate that a highly developed feminist consciousness, rather than a persisting conservatism, would lead women to downplay the importance of social class, because of

their awareness of the common problems facing women of all social classes. This kind of feminist analysis was not typical of women in Independencia. I believe the survey instead picked up a simple absence of class consciousness among women who would not display a strong gender consciousness either.

7. See, e.g., Paul L. Doughty, "Peruvian Migrant Identity in an Urban Milieu," in *The Anthropology of Urban Environments,* ed. T. Weaver and D. White (Boulder, Colo.: Society for Applied Anthropology, 1972); and Teófilo Altamirano, *La presencia andina en Lima* (Lima: Pontificia Universidad Católica del Perú, 1985).

8. See, e.g., Wayne Cornelius's treatment of migrants versus "native sons" in *Politics and the Migrant Poor in Mexico City* (Stanford: Stanford University Press, 1975).

9. The survey did not contain any questions eliciting respondents' racial characteristics or identification.

10. Path coefficients were derived by solving the following simultaneous structural equations:

$$X_1 = b_{12}X_2 + b_{13}X_3 + b_{14}X_4$$
$$X_2 = b_{23}X_3 + b_{25}X_5$$
$$X_3 = b_{34}X_4$$
$$X_4 = b_{45}X_5 + b_{46}X_6$$

where

X_1 = radicalism (dependent)
X_2 = union exposure
X_3 = male participation in local organizations
X_4 = educational achievement
X_5 = age
X_6 = sex

11. I assume that the system of relationships is recursive, that is, that no feedbacks or interactions among variables are at work.

12. In terms of our structural equations, the full impact of male participation is as follows:

$$b_{13} + (b_{12} \times b_{23}) = .138$$

I am assuming that involvement in local associations and clubs temporally precedes labor union membership in most men's lives, although the reverse may occur in some cases.

13. The direct impact of education on radicalism is represented by the path coefficient $b_{14} = .130$. But the full impact of education, when its impact on male participation is considered, is as follows:

$$b_{12} + (b_{13} \times b_{34}) = .144$$

14. The negative value of the path coefficient b_{46} reflects that the variable "sex" was scored as 1 for men and 2 for women.

15. This analysis of the impact of education clearly does not permit us to distinguish between two changes, both of which occurred under Velasco, namely, the *expansion* of educational opportunities for the poor and changes in the curricular *content*. Based on analysis of secondary sources and qualitative interviews with Independencia residents, I have concluded that both elements of the Velasco reforms, as well as the further changes in the content of education resulting from the radicalizing of the national teachers' union (see chapter 2) made education a key element in forging a more class-conscious and confrontational lower-class consciousness.

16. See Henry A. Dietz, "Political Participation in the Barriadas: An Extension and Reexamination," *Comparative Political Studies* 18, no. 3 (1985): 323–55; and Sandra Powell, "Political Participation in the Barriadas: A Case Study," ibid. 2, no. 2 (1969): 195–215. See also Maxwell A. Cameron, "Political Parties and the Worker-Employer Cleavage: The Impact of the Informal Sector on Voting in Lima, Peru". *Bulletin of Latin American Research* 10, no. 3 (1991): 293–313.

17. The simplification lies in combining Popular Action (AP) and the Popular Christian Party (PPC), two relatively conservative parties.

18. In 1985, one Las Flores resident explained, "we were between the Left and APRA. . . . The two groupings had almost the same principles of propaganda."

19. The percentage of respondents who voted "out of order"—e.g., they voted for the Left in 1985, say, but not in 1983—was 11.5 percent. This analysis includes only the 88.5 percent of respondents whose voting history corresponded to one of the five patterns described in table 13.

20. Similar results are obtained when support for the Left is measured over a series of elections. For example, of those scoring lowest in the measure of radicalism, only 14 percent voted consistently for the Left across these four elections, whereas 44 percent of the most radical consistently voted for the Left. In table 14 I have excluded voters who supported the more rightist PCP and AP candidates, because their numbers were very small.

21. In my fieldwork it was clear that many more women than men took part in church organizations. But the survey cannot confirm this, for very few respondents described themselves as members of any organizations (see question 20 on the survey instrument, in the appendix), including many respondents who went on the say they had taken active part in particular movements in the neighborhood (question 23). My sense is that people who an outsider might think of as members—because they attended meetings, took part in activities, etc.—did not think of themselves as members. They

may have thought of membership as entailing more formalized bonds, such as holding office in an organization or paying dues. It was therefore difficult to reach any conclusions on the relation between gender and the kinds of organizations respondents said they belonged to.

22. Path coefficients were derived by solving the following simultaneous equations:

$$X_1 = b_{12}X_2 + b_{13}X_3 + b_{16}X_6$$
$$X_2 = b_{24}X_4 + b_{25}X_5 + b_{27}X_7$$
$$X_3 = b_{35}X_5$$
$$X_4 = b_{47}X_7$$

where

X_1 = support for the Left in elections
X_2 = radicalism
X_3 = income
X_4 = unionism
X_5 = education
X_6 = female participation

23. Dietz, "Participation in the Barriadas."

Chapter 7

1. See David Collier and Ruth Berins Collier, "Inducements versus Constraints: Disaggregating 'Corporatism,'" *American Political Science Review* 73, no. 4 (1979): 967–86; and Alfred Stepan, *The State and Society: Peru in Comparative Perspective* (Princeton: Princeton University Press, 1978).

2. See Michael Taylor, "Rationality and Revolutionary Collective Action," in Taylor, ed., *Rationality and Revolution* (Cambridge: Cambridge University Press, 1988); Samuel Popkin, "Political Entrepreneurs and Peasant Movements in Vietnam," ibid.; and Dennis Chong, *Collective Action and the Civil Rights Movement* (Princeton: Princeton University Press, 1991).

3. Although I have followed Elster's definitions of irrationality, his examples of irrationality are individual-psychological, that is, they reflect cognitive limitations of the individual, but not distortions of beliefs flowing from the influence of the dominant. Thus, *sour grapes* is the tendency of individuals to downplay the desirability of things they desire but cannot have (which may be substantively irrational); *wishful thinking* is the tendency for individuals to adjust their beliefs to their desires (an instance of cognitive rationality); and individuals lack a cognitive grasp of statistical principles such as a return to the mean, leading, again, to cognitive irrationality. The sub-

stantive and cognitive irrationality I am describing flow not from individual psychology or cognitive "failures" but from social domination.

4. This is different from Elster's concept of *wishful thinking*—"the tendency to believe the facts are as one would like them to be"—in that the source of distortion he identifies is the passions (*Nuts and Bolts for the Social Sciences* [Cambridge: Cambridge University Press, 1989], 37). Here it is preexisting normative orientations that interfere with cognitive rationality.

5. James C. Scott, *Weapons of the Weak: Everyday Forms of Peasant Resistance* (New Haven: Yale University Press, 1985), 153–54, my emphasis.

6. Ibid., 164.

7. There is one exception: Mat "halus," a poor villager, offers a materialist interpretation of charity before double-cropping. He explains, "The well-off gave out *zakat peribadi* [a private Muslim tithe] so that they could call forth the work. . . . Poor people went everywhere. They called and we went" (ibid., 175). But this is the only materialist explanation of public liberality in the earlier era that I find in Scott's book.

8. Scott cites a study of credit in another village in the Muda Plain:

> Whenever village conversation was steered to the subject of mutual help and the offer of cash loans as part of such help to fellow villagers, it rarely failed to raise statements bemoaning the decreasing cooperation between villagers and the increasing difficulty of raising friendly loans. Such statements were *always accompanied* with reference to the fact that people in the village are becoming *increasingly calculating (berkira)* in their approach to money matters. Villagers would then unfailingly hark back to what was termed as the "old days" when people were always ready to offer aid.

(Mokhzani bin Abdul Rahim, "Credit in a Malay Peasant Society" [Ph.D. diss., University of London, 1973], emphasis Scott's, cited in ibid., 188). Because the Mokhzani study was carried out before the Green Revolution, it would seem to indicate a constant tendency for villagers to turn the past into the "good old days" and for the past to serve, as always, as a yardstick against which the present falls short (although this is not the inference Scott draws). But whether poor peasants hark back to some real period in their memory when they thought the rich were authentically generous or to a mythical past in which they think of the rich as having been authentically generous, it would seem that the poor think of their rich neighbors as authentically generous at some point in the past.

Seeing public liberality as reflecting the inherent traits of the adversary, not the broader problems posed by the (local) needs of economic production (such as labor scarcity), would also appear to be symptomatic of villagers' tendency, which Scott documents at length, toward personal, rather than social, explanations. And this turned out, again, to have been a mistaken interpretation. It is also one that we saw in Peru: poor people before the Velasco period, and a subset after, personalized the state. Recall one squatter's complaint about being bothered by "Señorita Gloria," the housing ministry official who tried repeatedly to evict squatters. Gloria was interpreted as a malevolent individual (which, of course, she may have been), but very little account was given to the state as a broader institution whose policies she was carrying out.

9. See esp. Gramsci's "Notes on Italian History," in *Selections from the Prison Notebooks,* ed. and trans. Quintin Hoare and Geoffrey Nowell Smith (New York: International Publishers, 1971).

10. Scott, *Weapons of the Weak,* 294, 301.

11. She is also not imagining a millenarian turning of the tables on the rich. Her imagined society, in which no one escapes the lot of the worst-off, is more different from her own experience than the millenarian dream, which tends to retain the actual features of society but makes the exploited the exploiters and vice versa.

12. Charles Tilly, introduction to *Class Conflict and Collective Action,* ed. Louise A. Tilly and Charles Tilly (Beverly Hills: Sage, 1981), 16.

13. Thus Gramsci wrote that the "social character [of schools] is determined by the fact that each social group has its own type of school, intended to perpetuate a specific traditional function, ruling or subordinate" ("On Education," *Selections from the Prison Notebooks,* 40).

14. For a discussion see Nicholas Abercrombie, Stephen Hill, and Bryan S. Turner, *The Dominant Ideology Thesis* (London: George Allen & Unwin, 1980).

15. Gramsci, "The Study of Philosophy," *Selections from the Prison Notebooks,* 333.

16. Scott, *Weapons of the Weak,* esp. chapter 8.

17. Gramsci, *Selections from the Prison Notebooks,* 327.

18. Stephan Lukes, *Power: A Radical View* (London: Macmillan, 1974), 47.

Postscript

1. The connection is not as fanciful as it might appear, since the accident was tied to the economic crisis, if not to "democracy." Short of cash, the Alianza Lima soccer team rented ill-maintained antique airplanes to travel to distant matches instead of taking commercial flights.

2. This is the result reported by Apoyo, a polling organization, in February 1991 (see their *Informe de Opinion,* February 1991). The survey was

of a stratified random sample of 612 adults in the Lima metropolitan area. The same survey asked respondents, "What does a policeman make you feel, security or fear?" Among respondents from the lowest socioeconomic stratum 59 percent felt fear and 32 percent, security (but among those from the wealthiest stratum 29 percent felt fear and 54 percent, security).

Bibliography

Abercrombie, Nicholas, Stephen Hill, and Bryan S. Turner. *The Dominant Ideology Thesis*. London: George Allen & Unwin, 1980.

Adrianzén, Alberto, ed. *Pensamiento político peruano: 1930–1968*. Lima: DESCO, 1990.

Altamirano, Teófilo. *La presencia andina en Lima*. Lima: Pontificia Universidad Católica del Perú, 1985.

Alvarez, Sonia. *Engendering Democracy in Brazil: Women's Movements in Transition Politics*. Princeton: Princeton University Press, 1990.

Americas Watch. *Abdicating Democratic Authority*. New York, 1984.

Anderson, Perry. "The Antinomies of Antonio Gramsci." *New Left Review* 100 (1977).

Andrews, Frank, and George W. Phillips. "The Squatters of Lima: Who They Are and What They Want." *Journal of Developing Areas* 4, no. 2 (1970).

Aramburú, Carlos Eduardo. *Migraciones internas: Perspectivas teóricas y metodológicas*. Lima: Instituto Andino de Estudios de Promoción y Desarrollo, 1981.

Arrellano Delgado, Nebiur. "La izquierda y los sindicatos." Bachelor's thesis, Universidad Nacional Federico Villareal, 1986.

Astiz, Carlos Alberto. "The Catholic Church in Politics: The Peruvian Case." *Ladoc,* March 1972.

Balbi, Carmen Rosa. *Identidad clasista en el sindicalismo*. Lima: DESCO, 1989.

———. *El Partido Comunista y el APRA en la crisis de los años treinta*. Lima: G. Herrera, 1980.

———. "La recesion silenciosa." *QuéHacer,* no. 59 (June–July 1989).

———. "Sindicalismo y caminos a la concertación." *Socialismo y Participación,* no. 38 (June 1987).

Banks, J. A. *The Sociology of Social Movements*. London: Macmillan, 1972.

Barrantes, Alfonso. *Barrantes: Sus propias palabras*. Lima: Mosca Azul, 1985.

Barrig, Maruja. *Convivir: La pareja en la pobreza*. Lima: Mosca Azul, 1982.

Basadre, Jorge. *Elecciones y centralismo en el Perú*. Lima: Centro de Investigación de la Universidad del Pacífico, 1980.

———. *Historia de la República del Perú, 1822–1933*. Vols. 8 and 9. Lima: Editorial Universitaria, 1968.

———. *Introducción a las bases documentales para la historia de la República del Perú*. Lima: P. L. Viueva, 1971.

Bergquist, Charles. *Labor in Latin America: Comparative Essays on Chile, Argentina, Venezuela, and Colombia*. Stanford: Stanford University Press, 1986.

Bernales, Enrique. *Movimientos sociales y movimientos universitarios en el Perú*. Lima: Pontificia Universidad Católica, 1975.

Bloch, Maurice. "The Past and the Present in the Present." *Man, the Journal of the Royal Anthropological Institute* 12, no. 2 (1977).

Blondet, Cecilia, Nicolás Lynch, and Carlos Iván Degregori. *Conquistadores de un nuevo mundo: De invasores a ciudadanos en San Martín de Porres*. Lima: Instituto de Estudios Peruanos, 1986.

Booth, David, and Bernardo Soj, eds. *Military Reformism and Social Classes: The Peruvian Experience, 1968–1980*. New York: St. Martin's Press, 1983.

Bourricaud, François. *Ideología y desarrollo: El caso del Partido Aprista Peruano*. Mexico City: El Colegio de Mexico, 1966.

Bright, Charles, and Susan Harding, eds. *Statemaking and Social Movements: Essays in History and Theory*. Ann Arbor: University of Michigan Press, 1984.

Burga, Manuel, and Alberto Flores Galindo. *Apogeo y crisis de la república aristocrática*. Lima: Ediciones Rikchay, 1980.

Burgos, Hernando. "Maestros: La ultima clase." *QuéHacer*, no. 58 (April 1989).

Calderón G., Fernando, ed. *Los movimientos sociales ante la crisis*. Buenos Aires: CLACSO, 1986.

Cameron, Maxwell A. "Political Parties and the Worker-Employer Cleavage: The Impact of the Informal Sector on Voting in Lima, Peru." *Bulletin of Latin American Research* 10, no. 3 (1991).

———. "The Politics of the Urban Informal Sector in Peru: Populism, Class, and 'Redistributive Combines.'" *Canadian Journal of Latin American and Caribbean Studies* 16, no. 31 (1991).

Canovan, Margaret. *Populism*. New York: Harcourt Brace Jovanovich, 1981.

Castells, Manuel. *The City and the Grassroots: A Cross-Cultural Theory of Urban Social Movements*. Berkeley and Los Angeles: University of California Press, 1983.

CEDAL. *La Federación Metalúrgica: Historia y problemas hoy (unidad sindical, clasismo, y partidos*. Lima, 1983.

Centro de Estudios de Población y Desarrollo. *Informe demográfico del Perú, 1970*. Lima, 1972.

Chang-Rodríguez, Eugenio. *Opciones políticas peruanas*. Lima: Centro de Documentación Andina, 1985.

Chong, Dennis. *Collective Action and the Civil Rights Movement*. Princeton: Princeton University Press, 1991.

CIPEP. *Informe*. Lima, n.d. Mimeographed.

CIPEP and Municipalidad de Lima, *Plan de emergencia distrital*. Lima: n.d. Mimeographed.

Clifford, James. *The Predicament of Culture*. Cambridge, Mass.: Cambridge University Press, 1988.

Cohen, Joshua, and Joel Rogers. "Secondary Associations and Democratic Governance." *Politics and Society* 20, no. 4 (1992).

Cohen, Youseff. *The Manipulation of Consent: The State and Working-Class Consciousness in Brazil*. Pittsburgh: University of Pittsburgh Press, 1989.

Collier, David. *Squatters and Oligarchs: Authoritarian Rule and Policy Change in Peru*. Baltimore: Johns Hopkins University Press, 1976.

Collier, David, and Ruth Berins Collier. "Inducements versus Constraints: Disaggregating 'Corporatism.'" *American Political Science Review* 73, no. 4 (1979).

———. *Shaping the Political Arena: Critical Junctures, the Labor Movement, and Regime Dynamics in Latin America*. Princeton: Princeton University Press, 1991.

Committee on Latin American Studies, University of California, Los Angeles. *Statistical Abstract of Latin America*. Vol. 25. Los Angeles: UCLA, 1987.

Conniff, Michael, ed. *Latin American Populism in Comparative Perspective*. Albuquerque: University of New Mexico Press, 1982.

Consejo Distrital de Independencia. *Boletín Municipal*. Nos. 1–5. Lima, 1986.

Cornelius, Wayne. *Politics and the Migrant Poor in Mexico City*. Stanford: Stanford University Press, 1975.

Cotler, Julio. *Clases, estado, y nación en el Perú*. Lima: Instituto de Estudios Peruanos, 1978.

———. "La crisis política, 1930–1968." in *Nueva historia general del Perú*, edited by Carlos Araníbar et al. Lima: Mosca Azul, 1979.

————. *Democracia e integración nacional.* Lima: Instituto de Estudios Peruanos, 1979.

Crenson, Mathew A. *The Un-Politics of Air Pollution: A Study of Non-Decisionmaking in the Cities.* Baltimore: Johns Hopkins Press, 1971.

Degregori, Carlos Iván. "Sendero Luminoso: Los hondos y mortales desencuentros." In *Movimientos sociales y crisis,* edited by Eduardo Ballón. Lima: DESCO, 1986.

Deustua, José, and Alberto Flores Galindo. "Los comunistas y el movimiento obrero: Perú, 1930–1931." In *Historia: Problema y promesa, homenaje a Jorge Basadre,* compiled by Francisco Miró Quesada. Lima: Pontificia Universidad Católica del Perú, 1978.

Deustua, José, Steve Stein, and Susan Stokes. "Soccer and Social Change in Early Twentieth-Century Peru." Pts. 1 and 2. *Journal of Latin American Popular Culture* 4 (1984) and 6 (1985).

Dietz, Henry A. "Bureaucratic Demand-Making and Clientelistic Participation in Peru." In *Authoritarianism and Corporatism in Latin America,* edited by James M. Malloy. Pittsburgh: University of Pittsburgh Press, 1977.

————. "Electoral Politics in Peru, 1978–1986." *Journal of InterAmerican Studies and World Affairs* 28 (winter 1986–87).

————. "Political Participation in the Barriadas: An Extension and Reexamination." *Comparative Political Studies* 18, no. 3 (1985).

————. *Poverty and Problem-Solving under Military Rule.* Austin: University of Texas Press, 1980.

Di Tella, Torcuato. "Populism and Reform in Latin America." In *Obstacles to Change in Latin America,* edited by Claudio Véliz. London: Oxford University Press, 1965.

Dix, Robert H. "Populism: Authoritarian and Democratic." *Latin American Research Review* 20, no. 2 (1985).

Dobyns, Henry, and Mario C. Vásquez, eds. *Migración e integración en el Perú.* Lima: Editorial Estudios Andinos, 1963.

Doughty, Paul L. "Peruvian Migrant Identity in an Urban Milieu." In *The Anthropology of Urban Environments,* edited by T. Weaver and D. White. Boulder, Colo.: Society for Applied Anthropology, 1972.

Drake, Paul W. *Socialism and Populism in Chile, 1932–52.* Urbana: University of Illinois Press, 1978.

Eckstein, Susan. *The Poverty of Revolution: The State and the Urban Poor in Mexico.* Princeton: Princeton University Press, 1977.

————. "Power and Popular Protest." In Eckstein, *Power and Popular Protest.*

————, ed. *Power and Popular Protest: Latin American Social Movements*. Berkeley and Los Angeles: University of California Press, 1989.

Eisenstadt, S. N., and L. Roniger. "Patron-Client Relations as a Model of Structuring Social Exchange." *Comparative Studies in Society and History* 22, no. 1 (1980).

Elster, Jon. *Cement of Society*. Cambridge: Cambridge University Press, 1989.

————. *Nuts and Bolts for the Social Sciences*. Cambridge: Cambridge University Press, 1989.

Escobar, Arturo, and Sonia Alvarez, eds. *The Making of Social Movements in Latin America*. Boulder, Colo.: Westview, 1992.

Eyerman, Ron, and Andrew Jamison. *Social Movements: A Cognitive Approach*. University Park: Pennsylvania State University Press, 1991.

Femia, Joseph. "Hegemony and Consciousness in the Thought of Antonio Gramsci." *Political Studies* 23, no. 1 (1975).

FitzGerald, E. V. K. *The Political Economy of Peru, 1956–78*. Cambridge: Cambridge University Press, 1979.

Flores Galindo, Alberto. *La agonía de Mariátegui: La polémica con el Komintern*. Lima: Mosca Azul, 1980.

————. "La generación del '68: Ilusión y realidad." *Márgenes: Encuentro y Debate* 1, no. 1 (1987).

————. "La guerra silenciosa." In Flores Galindo and Manrique, *Violencia y campesinado*.

————. "Prólogo." *El pensamiento comunista*. Lima: Mosca Azul, 1982.

Flores Galindo, Alberto, and Nelson Manrique. *Violencia y campesinado*. Lima: Instituto de Apoyo Agrario, 1986.

Foweracker, Joe. *Making Democracy in Spain: Grass-Roots Struggle in the South, 1955–1975*. Cambridge: Cambridge University Press, 1989.

Franco, Carlos. *Perú: Participación popular*. Lima: Centro de Estudios sobre el Desarrollo y la Participación, 1979.

Fried, Jacob. "Acculturation and Mental Health among Indian Migrants in Peru." In *Culture and Mental Health*, edited by M. K. Opler. New York: Macmillan, 1959.

Fukumoto Soto, Mary. *Relaciones raciales en un tugurio de Lima: El caso de huerta perdida*. Master's thesis, Pontificia Universidad Católica de Lima, 1976.

Galeano, Luis. "Entre la protesta y la lucha urbana." *Revista Paraguaya de Sociología* 23, no. 66 (1986).

Galín, Pedro, Julio Carrión, and Oscar Castillo. *Asalariados y clases populares en Lima*. Lima: Instituto de Estudios Peruanos, 1986.

García Guerra, Francisco. *Velasco: Del estado oligárquico al capitalismo del estado*. Lima: Centro de Estudios para el Desarrollo y la Participación, 1983.

Garretón, Manuel Antonio. "Popular Mobilization and the Military Regime in Chile: The Complexities of the Invisible Transition." In Eckstein, *Power and Popular Protest*.

Gaventa, John. *Power and Powerlessness: Quiescence and Rebellion in an Appalachian Valley*. Urbana: University of Illinois Press, 1980.

Geertz, Clifford. *The Interpretation of Cultures*. New York: Basic Books, 1973.

Gelner, Ernest, and Ghita Ionescu, eds. *Populism: Its Meanings and National Character*. London: Weidenfeld & Nicholson, 1969.

Giddens, Anthony. *Central Problems in Social Theory: Action, Structure, and Contradiction in Social Analysis*. London: Macmillan, 1979.

Goldrich, Daniel. "Political Organization and the Politicization of the Poblador." *Comparative Political Studies* 3, no. 2 (1970).

González, Raúl. "Ayacucho en el año de Noel." *QuéHacer* no. 27 (February 1984).

Gorman, Stephen M. *Post-Revolutionary Peru: The Politics of Transformation*. Boulder, Colo.: Westview, 1982.

Graham, Carol L. *Peru's APRA: Parties, Politics, and the Elusive Quest for Democracy*. Boulder, Colo.: Lynne Rienner, 1992.

Gramsci, Antonio. *Selections from the Prison Notebooks*. Edited and translated by Quintin Hoare and Geoffrey Nowell Smith. New York: International Publishers, 1971.

Grupo Warmi. *Informe anual*. Lima, 1984.

Guerrero de los Ríos, Raul, and Abelardo Sánchez León. *La trampa urbana; ideología y problemas urbanos: El caso de Lima*. Lima: DESCO, 1977.

Habermas, Jürgen. *Communication and the Evolution of Society*. Translated by Thomas McCarthy. Boston: Beacon, 1976.

———. *Legitimation Crisis*. Translated by Thomas McCarthy. Boston: Beacon, 1975.

Hale, Charles R. *Resistance and Contradiction: Miskitu Indians and the Nicaraguan State, 1894–1987*. Stanford: Stanford University Press, 1994.

Hall, Stuart, Dorothy Hobson, Andrew Lowe, and Paul Willis, eds. *Culture, Media, Language*. London: Hutchinson, 1980.

Hall, Stuart, Bob Lumley, and Gregor McLennan. "Politics and Ideology: Gramsci." In *On Ideology*, edited by the Centre for Contemporary Cultural Studies. London: Hutchinson, 1977.

Henríquez, Narda, and Ana Ponce. *Lima: Población, trabajo, y política.* Lima: Pontificia Universidad Católica del Perú, 1985.

Henry, Etienne. *La escena urbana: Estado y movimientos de pobladores, 1968–1976.* Lima: Pontificia Universidad Católica del Perú, 1978.

Hirschman, Albert. *The Passions and the Interests: Political Arguments for Capitalism before Its Triumph.* Princeton: Princeton University Press, 1977.

Hunt, Shane. "Distribution, Growth, and Government Economic Behavior in Peru." In *Government and Economic Behavior,* edited by Gustav Rains. New Haven: Yale University Press, 1971.

Huntington, Samuel P. *Political Order in Changing Societies.* New Haven: Yale University Press, 1968.

Informe demográfico del Perú. Lima: Centro de Estudios de Población y Desarrollo, 1972.

Instituto Nacional de Estadística. *VIII Censo Nacional de Población y III de Vivienda 1981, Departamento de Lima.* Lima, 1981.

Isbell, Billie Jean. "The Influence of Migrants upon Traditional Social and Political Concepts: A Peruvian Case Study." In *Latin American Urban Research,* vol. 4, *Anthropological Perspectives on Latin American Urbanization,* edited by Wayne A. Cornelius and Felicity M. Trueblood. Beverly Hills: Sage, 1974.

Jaquette, Jane S., ed. *The Women's Movement in Latin America: Feminism and the Transition to Democracy.* Winchester, Mass.: Unwin Hyman, 1989.

Jelin, Elizabeth, ed. *Movimientos sociales y democracia emergente.* 2 vols. Buenos Aires: Centro Editor de América Latina, 1987.

———. *Los nuevos movimientos sociales.* 2 vols. Buenos Aires: Centro Editor de América Latina, 1985.

Johnson, John J. *Political Change in Latin America: The Emergence of the Middle Sectors.* Stanford: Stanford University Press, 1958.

Karl, Terry Lynn. "Dilemmas of Democracy in Latin America." *Comparative Politics* 23, no. 1 (1990).

Kaufman, Robert R. "Corporatism, Clientelism, and Partisan Conflict: A Study of Seven Latin American Countries." In *Authoritarianism and Corporatism in Latin America,* edited by James M. Malloy. Pittsburgh: University of Pittsburgh Press, 1977.

Klaiber, Jeffrey, S.J. "The González Prada Popular Universities and the Origins of Aprismo, 1921–24." *Hispanic American Historical Review* 55, no. 4 (1975).

———. *Religion and Revolution in Peru, 1824–1976.* Notre Dame: University of Notre Dame Press, 1977.

Klandermans, Bert, Hanspeter Kriesi, and Sidney Tarrow, eds. *From Structure to Action: Comparing Social Movements across Cultures.* Greenwich, Conn.: JAI, 1988.

Klarén, Peter. *Modernization, Dislocation, and Aprismo: Origins of the Peruvian Aprista Party, 1870–1932.* Austin: University of Texas Press, 1973.

LaClau, Ernesto. *Politics and Ideology in Marxist Theory.* London: New Left Books, 1972.

Lago, Ricardo. "The Illusion of Pursuing Redistribution through Macropolicy: Peru's Heterodox Experience, 1985–1990." In *The Macroeconomics of Populism in Latin America,* edited by Rudiger Dornbusch and Sebastian Edwards. Chicago: University of Chicago Press, 1991.

Laitin, David D. *Hegemony and Culture: Politics and Religious Change among the Yoruba.* Chicago: University of Chicago Press, 1986.

Landé, Carl H. "The Dyadic Basis of Clientelism." In Schmidt et al., *Friends, Followers, and Factions: A Reader in Political Clientelism.*

Larrain, Jorge. *Marxism and Ideology.* London: Macmillan, 1983.

Leeds, Anthony. "The Concept of the 'Culture of Poverty': Conceptual, Logical, and Empirical Problems, with Perspectives from Brazil and Peru." In *The Culture of Poverty: A Critique,* edited by E. Leacock. New York: Simon & Schuster, 1971.

Leeds, Anthony, and Elizabeth Leeds. "Brazil and the Myth of Urban Rurality: Urban Experience, Work, and Values in 'Squatments' of Rio de Janeiro and Lima." In *City and Country in the Third World: Issues in the Modernization of Latin America,* edited by Arthur J. Field. Cambridge: Schenkman, 1970.

Léon García, Enrique. *Las razas de Lima.* Lima: Universidad Mayor de San Marcos, 1909.

Letts, Ricardo. *La izquierda peruana: Organizaciones y tendencias.* Lima: Mosca Azul, 1981.

Levine, Daniel H. "Religion and Politics: Drawing Lines, Understanding Change." *Latin American Research Review* 20, no. 1 (1985).

——, ed. *Religion and Political Conflict in Latin America.* Chapel Hill: University of North Carolina Press, 1986.

Lobo, Susan. *A House of My Own: Social Organization in the Squatter Settlements of Lima, Peru.* Tucson: University of Tucson Press, 1982.

Lomnitz, Larissa. *Networks and Marginality: Life in a Mexican Shantytown.* New York: Academic, 1977.

Lowenthal, Abraham, ed. *The Peruvian Experiment: Continuity and Change under Military Rule.* Princeton: Princeton University Press, 1975.

Lowenthal, Abraham, and Cynthia McClintock, eds. *The Peruvian Experiment Reconsidered.* Princeton: Princeton University Press, 1983.

Lukes, Stephen. *Power: A Radical View.* London: Macmillan, 1974.

Lustic, Ian. "Becoming Problematic: Breakdown of a Hegemonic Conception of Ireland in Nineteenth-Century Britain." *Politics and Society* 18, no. 1 (1990).

McAdam, Doug. *Political Process and the Development of Black Insurgency, 1930–1970.* Chicago: University of Chicago Press, 1982.

McCarthy, John D., and Meyer N. Zald. "Resource Mobilization and Social Movements: A Partial Theory." *American Journal of Sociology* 82 (1977).

McClintock, Cynthia. *Peasant Cooperatives and Political Change in Peru.* Princeton: Princeton University Press, 1981.

———. "Peru's Sendero Luminoso Rebellion: Origins and Trajectory." In Eckstein, *Power and Popular Protest.*

———. "Prospects for Democratic Consolidation in a 'Least Likely' Case." *Comparative Politics* 21 (January 1989).

———. "Why Peasants Rebel: The Case of Peru's Sendero Luminoso." *World Politics* 37 (1984).

Mainwaring, Scott. "Brazil: The Catholic Church and the Popular Movement in Nova Iguaçu, 1974–1985." In Levine, *Religion and Political Conflict in Latin America.*

———. *The Catholic Church and Politics in Brazil, 1916–1985.* Stanford: Stanford University Press, 1986.

Mainwaring, Scott, and Eduardo Viola. "New Social Movements, Political Culture, and Democracy: Brazil and Argentina in the 1980s." *Telos* 17, no. 3 (1984).

Mangin, William P. "Latin American Squatter Settlements: A Problem and a Solution." *Latin American Research Review* 2, no. 3 (1967).

———. "Mental Health and Migration to Cities: A Peruvian Case." *Annals of the New York Academy of Sciences* 84 (1960).

———. "Similarities and Differences between Two Types of Peruvian Communities." *Sociologus* 16, no. 1 (1965).

———. "Sociological, Cultural, and Political Characteristics of Some Urban Migrants in Peru." In *Urban Anthropology: Cross-Cultural Studies of Urbanization,* edited by Aidan Southall. New York: Oxford University Press, 1973.

———. "Squatter Settlements." *Scientific American* 217, no. 4 (1967).

———, ed. *Peasants in Cities: Readings in the Anthropology of Urbanization.* Boston: Houghton Mifflin, 1970.

Marx, Karl, and Friedrich Engels. *The German Ideology.* Edited and translated by R. Pascal. New York: International Publishers, 1947.

Matos Mar, José. *Las barriadas de Lima, 1957.* Lima: Instituto de Estudios Peruanos, 1967.

———. *Crisis del estado y desborde popular.* 2d ed. Lima: Instituto de Estudios Peruanos, 1986.

Melucci, Alberto. *Nomads of the Present: Social Movements and Individual Needs in Contemporary Society.* Philadelphia: Temple University Press, 1989.

Michl, Sara. "Urban Squatter Organization as a National Government Tool: The Case of Lima, Peru." In *Latin American Urban Research,* vol. 3, *National-Local Linkages: The Inter-Relationships of Urban and National Policies in Latin America.* Beverly Hills: Sage, 1973.

Millones, Luis. *Tugurio, la cultura de los marginados.* Lima: Instituto Nacional de Cultura, 1978.

Moore, Barrington. *Injustice: The Social Bases of Obedience and Revolt.* London: Macmillan, 1978.

Moreira Alves, Maria Helena. "Interclass Alliances and the Opposition to the Military in Brazil: Consequences for the Transition Period." In Eckstein, *Power and Popular Protest.*

Mouzelis, Nicos. "On the Concept of Populism: Populist and Clientelist Modes of Incorporation in Semiperipheral Polities." *Politics and Society* 14, no. 3 (1985).

Munck, Gerardo. "Social Movements and Democracy in Latin America: Theoretical Debates and Comparative Perspectives." Paper presented at the Sixteenth Congress of the Latin American Studies Association, Washington, D.C., April 1991.

Municipalidad de Independencia. *Plan de desarrollo integral del distrito de Independencia.* Lima: n.d. Mimeographed.

North, Liisa, and Tanya Korovkin. *The Peruvian Revolution and the Officers in Power.* Montreal: McGill Centre for Developing-Area Studies, 1981.

O'Donnell, Guillermo. "Corporatism and the Question of the State." In *Authoritarianism and Corporatism in Latin America,* edited by James M. Malloy. Pittsburgh: University of Pittsburgh Press, 1977.

———. *Modernization and Bureaucratic-Authoritarianism: Studies in South American Politics.* Berkeley: Institute of International Studies, 1973.

O'Donnell, Guillermo, and Philippe C. Schmitter. *Transitions from Authoritarian Rule: Tentative Conclusions about Uncertain Democracies.* Baltimore: Johns Hopkins University Press, 1986.

Offe, Claus. "Challenging the Boundaries of Institutional Politics." In *Changing Boundaries of the Political,* edited by Charles S. Maier. Cambridge: Cambridge University Press, 1987.

Olson, Mancur. *The Logic of Collective Action*. Cambridge: Harvard University Press, 1971.

Opp, Karl-Dieter. *The Rationality of Political Protest: A Comparative Analysis of Rational Choice Theory*. Boulder, Colo.: Westview, 1989.

Osterling, Jorge P. *De campesinado a profesional: Migrantes de Huayopampa en Lima*. Lima: Pontificia Universidad Católica del Perú, 1980.

Oxhorn, Philip. *Organizaciones poblacionales: La reconstitución de la sociedad civil y la interacción elite-base*. Santiago: Centro de Estudios Sociales, 1987.

Palmer, David Scott. *Peru: The Authoritarian Tradition*. New York: Praeger, 1980.

———. "'Revolution from Above': Military Government and Popular Participation." Ph.D. diss., Cornell University, 1973.

———, ed. *The Shining Path of Peru*. New York: St. Martin's, 1992.

Panfichi, Aldo. "La crisis y las multitudes: Lima, 5 de febrero de 1975." *Debates en Sociología*, no. 9 (1983).

Pareja, Piedad. *Anarquismo y sindicalismo en el Perú (1904–1929)*. Lima: Ediciones Rikchay, 1978.

Parodi, Jorge. "La desmovilización del sindicalismo industrial peruano en el segundo belaundismo." In *Movimientos sociales y crisis*, edited by Eduardo Ballón. Lima: DESCO, 1986.

———. *Ser obrero es algo relativo*. Lima: Instituto de Estudios Peruanos, 1986.

Pásara, Luis. *Radicalización y conflicto en la iglesia peruana*. Lima: El Virrey, 1986.

Patch, Richard. "Life in a *Callejón*: A Study of Urban Disorganization." *American Universities Field Staff Reports* 8, no. 6 (1961).

———. "La Parada, Lima's Market: A Study of Class and Assimilation." *American Universities Field Staff Reports* 14, nos. 1–3 (1967).

Pease García, Henry. *Los caminos al poder: Tres años de crisis en la escena política*. Lima: DESCO, 1979.

———. *El ocaso del poder oligárquico: Lucha política en la escena oficial, 1968–75*. Lima: DESCO, 1977.

Perlman, Janet. *The Myth of Marginality: Urban Politics in Rio de Janeiro*. Berkeley: Campus Books, 1976.

Piven, Frances Fox, and Richard A. Cloward. *Poor People's Movements: Why They Succeed, How They Fail*. New York: Pantheon, 1977.

Popkin, Samuel. "Political Entrepreneurs and Peasant Movements in Vietnam." In *Rationality and Revolution*, edited by Michael Taylor. Cambridge: Cambridge University Press, 1988.

———. *The Rational Peasant: The Political Economy of Rural Society in Vietnam*. Berkeley and Los Angeles: University of California Press, 1979.

Portocarrero, Gonzálo. *De Bustamante a Odría: El fracaso del Frente Democrático Nacional, 1945–1950*. Lima: Mosca Azul, 1983.

———. "Los fantasmas de la clase media." *Hueso Húmero*, no. 20 (1986).

Portocarrero, Gonzálo, and Patricia Oliart. *El Perú desde la escuela*. Lima: Instituto de Apoyo Agrario, 1986.

Powell, Sandra. "Political Participation in the Barriadas: A Case Study." *Comparative Political Studies* 2, no. 2 (1969).

Przeworski, Adam. *Capitalism and Social Democracy*. Cambridge: Cambridge University Press, 1985.

———. *The State and the Economy under Capitalism*. Chur, Switzerland: Harwood Academic Publishers, 1990.

Przeworski, Adam, and John Sprague. *Paper Stones: A History of Electoral Socialism*. Chicago: University of Chicago Press, 1986.

Quijano, Aníbal. *Imperialismo y "marginalidad" en América Latina*. Lima: Mosca Azul Editores, 1977.

Revilla, Julio. "Industrialización temprana y lucha ideológica en el Perú: 1890–1910." *Estudios Andinos*, nos. 17–18 (1981).

Reynoso, Oswaldo, Vilma Aguilar, and Hildebrado Perez H. *Luchas del magisterio: De Mariátegui al SUTEP*. Lima: Ediciones Narración, 1979.

Riofrío, Gustavo. *Se busca terreno para próxima barriada; espacios disponibles en Lima, 1940–1978–1990*. Lima: DESCO, 1978.

Riofrío, Gustavo, and Alfredo Rodríguez. *De invasores a invadidos*. 2d ed. Lima: DESCO, 1980.

Romero, Catalina. "Cambios en la relación iglesia-sociedad en el Perú." *Debates en Sociología*, no. 7 (1986).

Roncagliolo, Rafael. *Quién ganó? Elecciones, 1931–1980*. Lima: DESCO, 1980.

Rospigliosi, Fernando. *Los jóvenes obreros de los '80: Inseguridad, eventualidad, y radicalismo*. Lima: Instituto de Estudios Peruanos, 1987.

Rummel, R. J. *Applied Factor Analysis*. Evanston, Ill.: Northwestern University Press, 1970.

Sahlins, Marshall. *Culture and Practical Reason*. Chicago: University of Chicago Press, 1976.

Sanborn, Cynthia. "The Democratic Left and the Persistence of Populism in Peru," 1975–1990. Ph.D. diss., Harvard University, 1991.

Schmidt, Steffan W., Laura Guasti, Carl H. Landé, and James C. Scott, eds. *Friends, Followers, and Factions: A Reader in Political Clientelism*. Berkeley and Los Angeles: University of California Press, 1977.

Schmitter, Philippe C. *Interest Conflict and Political Change in Brazil.* Stanford: Stanford University Press, 1971.

———. "Paths to Political Development in Latin America." In *Changing Latin America,* edited by Douglas A. Chalmers. New York: Academy of Political Science, Columbia University, 1972.

———. *Patterns of Corporatist Policy-Making,* Beverly Hills: Sage, 1982.

———. "Still the Century of Corporatism?" In *The New Corporatism: Social-Political Structures in the Iberian World,* edited by Frederick B. Pike and Thomas Stritch. Notre Dame: University of Notre Dame Press, 1974.

Schmitter, Philippe, and Terry Lynn Karl. "What Democracy Is . . . and Is Not." *Journal of Democracy* 2, no. 3 (1991).

Scott, James C. *Domination and the Arts of Resistance: Hidden Transcripts.* New Haven: Yale University Press, 1990.

———. *Weapons of the Weak: Everyday Forms of Peasant Resistance.* New Haven: Yale University Press, 1985.

Scurrah, Martin. "Military Reformism in Peru: Opening the Pandora's Box." *Latin American Research Review* 21, no. 1 (1986).

Simmons, Ozzie G. "The Criollo Outlook in the Mestizo Culture of Coastal Peru." *American Anthropologist* 57 (1955).

Skocpol, Theda. "Bringing the State Back In: Strategies of Analysis in Current Research." In *Bringing the State Back In,* edited by Peter B. Evans, Dietrich Rueschemeyer, and Theda Skocpol. Cambridge: Cambridge University Press, 1985.

———. *States and Social Revolutions: A Comparative Analysis of France, Russia, and China.* Cambridge: Cambridge University Press, 1979.

Slater, David, ed. *New Social Movements and the State in Latin America.* Amsterdam: CEDLA, 1985.

Stallings, Barbara. *Banker to the Third World: U.S. Portfolio Investment in Latin America, 1900–1986.* Berkeley and Los Angeles: University of California Press, 1987.

———. "International Capitalism and the Peruvian Military Government." In Lowenthal and McClintock, *The Peruvian Experiment Reconsidered.*

———. "Peru and the U.S. Banks: Privatization of Financial Relations." In *Capitalism and the State in U.S.–Latin American Relations,* edited by Richard R. Fagen. Stanford: Stanford University Press, 1979.

Starn, Orin. "'I Dreamed of Foxes and Hawks': Reflections on Peasant Protest, New Social Movements, and the *Rondas Campesinas* of Northern Peru." In Escobar and Alvarez, *The Making of Social Movements in Latin America.*

―――. "New Literature on Peru's Sendero Luminoso." *Latin American Research Review* 27, no. 2 (1992).

Stein, Steve. "Populism and Mass Politics in Peru: The Political Behavior of the Working Classes in the 1931 Presidential Election." Ph.D. diss., Stanford University, 1973.

―――. *Populism in Peru: The Emergence of the Masses and the Politics of Social Control.* Madison: University of Wisconsin Press, 1980.

―――. "El vals criollo y los valores de la clase trabajadora en la Lima de comienzos del siglo XX." *Socialismo y Participación,* no. 17 (March 1982).

―――, ed. *Lima obrera: 1900–1930.* 2 vols. Lima: El Virrey, 1985–1987.

Stepan, Alfred. *The State and Society: Peru in Comparative Perspective.* Princeton: Princeton University Press, 1978.

Stephens, Evelyn Huber. "The Peruvian Military Government, Labor Mobilization, and the Political Strength of the Left." *Latin American Research Review* 18, no. 2 (1983).

―――. *The Politics of Workers' Participation: The Peruvian Approach in Comparative Perspective.* New York: Academic, 1980.

Stokes, Susan C. "Hegemony, Consciousness, and Political Change in Peru." *Politics and Society* 19, no. 3 (1991).

―――. "Politics and Latin America's Urban Poor: Notes from a Lima Shantytown." *Latin American Research Review* 26, no. 2 (1991).

―――. "Raza y clase social: Los afro-peruanos de Lima." In Stein, *Lima obrera,* vol. 2.

Sulmont, Denis. "Crisis, huelgas, y movimientos populares urbanos en el Perú." *Debates en Sociología,* no. 3 (1978).

―――. *El movimiento obrero en el Perú, 1890–1980.* Lima: Tarea, 1980.

Tarrow, Sidney. *Democracy and Disorder: Protest and Politics in Italy, 1965–1975.* Oxford: Clarendon, 1989.

Taylor, Michael. "Rationality and Revolutionary Collective Action." In *Rationality and Revolution,* edited by Michael Taylor. Cambridge: Cambridge University Press, 1988.

Tejada R., Luis. *La cuestión del pan.* Lima: Instituto Nacional de Cultura, 1988.

Thompson, E. P. *The Making of the English Working Class.* Harmondsworth: Pelican, 1982.

―――. "The Moral Economy of the English Crowd in the Eighteenth Century." *Past and Present,* no. 50 (1971).

Thorndike, Guillermo. *El año de la barbarie.* Lima: Nueva América, 1969.

Thorp, Rosemary. "Políticas de ajuste en el Perú, 1956–1985: Los efectos de una crisis." *Economía* 7, no. 14 (1984).

Thorp, Rosemary, and Geoffrey Bertram. *Peru, 1890–1977: Growth and Policy in an Open Economy*. London: Macmillan, 1978.

Tilly, Charles. *From Mobilization to Revolution*. Reading, Mass.: Addison-Wesley, 1978.

————. "Models and Realities of Popular Collective Action." *Social Research* 52 (1985).

Tilly, Charles, and Louise A. Tilly, eds. *Class Conflict and Collective Action*. Beverly Hills: Sage, 1981.

Touraine, Alain. *Actores sociales y sistemas políticos en América Latina*. Santiago: PREALC/OIT, 1987.

Tovar, Teresa. *Reforma de la educación: Balance y perspectiva*. Lima: DESCO, 1985.

————. *Velasquismo y movimiento popular: Historia del movimiento popular, 1968–1975*. Lima: DESCO, 1986.

Trimberger, Ellen Kay. *Revolution from Above: Military Bureaucracies and Development in Japan, Turkey, Egypt, and Peru*. New Brunswick, N.J.: Transaction Books, 1978.

Tuesta Soldevilla, Fernando. *Elecciones municipales: Cifras y escenario político*. Lima: DESCO, 1983.

————. *El nuevo rostro electoral: Las municipales del '83*. Lima: DESCO, 1985.

————. *Perú político en cifras: Elite política y elecciones*. Lima: Fundación Friedrich Ebert, 1987.

————. *Pobreza urbana y cambios electorales en Lima*. Lima: DESCO, 1989.

Uzzell, John D. "Cholos and Bureaus in Lima: A Case History and Analysis." *International Journal of Comparative Sociology* 15, nos. 3–4 (1974).

————. "A Strategic Analysis of Social Structure in Lima: Using the Concept of 'Plays.'" *Urban Anthropology* 3, no. 1 (1974).

Vilas, Carlos. "El sujeto social de la insurrección popular: La revolución Sandinista." *Latin American Research Review* 20, no. 1 (1985).

Villanueva, Víctor. *El APRA en busca del poder*. Lima: Editorial Horizonte, 1975.

————. *El ejército peruano, del caudillaje anárquico al militarismo reformista*. Lima: Editorial Juan Mejía Baca, 1973.

Wallace, James M. "Urban Anthropology in Lima: An Overview." *Latin American Research Review* 19, no. 3 (1984).

Walton, John. "Debt, Protest, and the State in Latin America." In Eckstein, *Power and Popular Protest*.

————. *Reluctant Rebels*. New York: Columbia University Press, 1984.

Weber, Max. *Max Weber: The Theory of Social and Economic Organization*. Edited by Talcott Parsons. New York: Free Press, 1964 [1947].

Wise, Carol. "Peru Post-1968: The Political Limits to State-Led Economic Development." Ph.D. diss., Columbia University, 1990.

Yepes del Castillo, Ernesto. "El desarrollo peruano en las primeras décadas del siglo XX." In *Nueva historia general del Perú*, by Carlos Araníbar et al. Lima: Mosca Azul, 1979.

———. *Perú 1820–1920: Un siglo de desarrollo capitalista*. Lima: Instituto de Estudios Peruanos, 1972.

Yepes del Castillo, Isabel, and Jorge Bernedo Alvarez. *La sindicalización en el Perú*. Lima: Fundación Ebert and Pontificia Universidad Católica del Perú, 1985.

Zaluar, Alba. *A máquina e a revolta: As organizacoes populares e o significado da pobreza*. São Paulo: Editora Brasilense, 1985.

Index

APRA, 17–18, 20, 52; government of Alan García, 40, 61; in Independencia, 30; and labor, 35, 69, 113; and land invasions, 24; in 1985 elections, 101, 105. *See also* Political parties

Balbi, Carmen Rosa, 34
Barrantes, Alfonso, 49, 55, 101
Belaúnde Terry, Fernando, 26, 32, 56; first administration, 29. *See also* Popular Action
Beltrán, Pedro, 26, 76, 126
Blanco, Hugo, 150n7
Bondy, Salazar, 150n7

Catholic church: Episcopal Council of, 154n8; and Left, 57, 107; during the oligarchic state, 19; and participation, 72–73; and Velasco regime, 39, 40, 57–58, 153n27
Change 90 (Cambio 90), 49, 52
Clientelism, 15, 16, 30; definition of, 55, 112; in Independencia, 55–58; and Left, 43; and the oligarchic state, 18, 22; as a pattern of political culture, 62–84 passim
Collier, David, 26, 148nn24, 25
Committee to Promote Development (Comité de Promoción delesarrollo, COPRODE), 37, 41
Communist Party, 17, 40, 150n7; in Independencia, 30; and labor, 35, 69, 151n19; and Velasco regime, 35, 153n26. *See also* Left

Consciousness, 124; and the Church, 57; and counterhegemony, 131; "false," 122, 129; in Gramsci, 7, 130; of social class, 66–71, 73, 81. *See also* Culture; Hegemony
Confederation of Peruvian Workers (Confederación de Trabajadores del Perú, CTP), 35
Consent and social order, 5, 10
Corporatism, 12, 113–115; inclusionary and exclusionary, 33, 42
CRAV (Commission for Agrarian and Housing Reform), 26
Culture: and domination, 8, 9; and norms, 120; and the oligarchic state, 18–20; state intervention in, 11. *See also* Hegemony

Delgado, Carlos, 37, 38
Democracy, 51, 133, 135–136, 162n1
Dietz, Henry, 22, 36, 37, 38, 100, 108–109
Directorate of Young People (Dirrección de Pueblos Jóvenes, DPJ), 38

Education: and gender, 99; and Left, 45, 107–108, 153n31; during the oligarchic state, 19; and political culture, 98–99; under Velasco regime, 38, 45, 73, 92, 159n15
Elections: of 1931, 21; in 1960s, 21; in 1980s, 22, 48–49. *See also* Voting behavior
Elster, Jon, 120, 160n3, 161n4
Engels, Friedrich, 7